Human Resources A to Z

Human Resources A to Z

A Practical Field Guide for People Managers

Ted Smith

Edward MR Smith

CONTENTS ▌

CONTENTS

CONTENTS

CONTENTS

CONTENTS

CONTENTS

CONTENTS

CONTENTS

This book is dedicated to Joan Yearwood, who hails from Barbados. Joan originally worked as a clippie on the old Number 9 bus route between Barnes and Liverpool Street, serving the theatres and St Pauls School. She tells everyone that she then worked for Henry Wellcome. I believe her, even if no-one else does. When I worked at Wellcome Trust, she always found a way to make me smile. Every single day. Joan is one of those rare people that cloning was invented for and we did try to clone her, when she allowed us to make a 3D model of her for the Joannie Award (given annually to the outstanding member of the Facilities team)

Introduction

My training in Human Resources at college was distinctly average. The biggest problem was that the teaching was academically based, and lacked any real connection with the world I was working in. Often my textbooks suggested a simple black-and-white answer, but human beings are all different, with individual motivations, and they all deserve to be listened to and treated with respect.

To keep me out of mischief, one of my first line managers asked me to update the company handbook. A month later, I had converted the handbook from a set of rules ('You will phone in sick before 8 am, or you will not receive sick pay') to some guidelines ('When you need to take sick leave, please try to contact your line manager, or a colleague, as soon as you are able to'). Thankfully, the COO loved the new guidelines and I got a promotion instead of the sack. Ever since then, I have worked towards offering sensible and sensitive guidance, rather than a didactic, one-size-fits-all response.

This book is a collection of practical ideas and ways of getting stuff done. Hopefully, you can learn from my mistakes and make a real difference in HR, as a consequence of reading some of these tips and tricks of the trade. I suggest you have a quick skim through all the pages to get an idea of how the A to Z system works, then dip in and out of the book as needs dictate. Some sections will be useful as a standard tool in your armoury; others will only be needed when an issue arises.

TED SMITH

All about me

So, where did my interest in all things HR stem from? Way back in time, I worked on the picking line at a biscuit factory to earn some summer holiday money. After a week, the management decided they wanted us to have fewer breaks from the tedious job of watching out for a broken biscuit and throwing it in a bag behind us. Instead of five minutes every hour, we were going to get seven minutes mid-morning and another seven minutes mid-afternoon to go to the loo, or 'take a fag break', as it was known in those days. This is when I learned my first lesson about how it feels not to be consulted or engaged. The announcement was made at 8 am as the shift started, with no prior warning. We were going to have a break at 10 am and then lunch as normal at 1 pm (unpaid of course), rather than breaks at 09.00, 10.15 and 11.30 am. No one was amused, but we all got on with it.

At 9 am the alarms went off, signifying that a foreign body had entered the packaging line, and production came to a speedy halt. The Quality Control Manager arrived, and after much muttering and poking around in the machinery, he found a small bolt. We enjoyed our extended break whilst he sorted it all out, and started again without complaint. Strangely, the very same thing happened at 10.15 am, and then at 11.30 am. Over lunch we learned that a paper clip had somehow found its way into the line, and then a drawing pin. The management team were seen congregating in a corner. After lunch there was an announcement, followed by an almighty cheer, when they told us that the old breaks were being reinstated with immediate effect. The power of the people.

Whilst studying for an environmental science degree at Leicester Polytechnic, I got involved in the Students' Union, setting up new sports clubs and helping out with the student newspaper, *PRUNE* (Polytechnic Rubbish, Unions News and Events). I was later elected to the sabbatical role of VP Academic Affairs, which involved helping students who were struggling with visas and coursework. Having come from a semi-privileged white upbringing in the white suburbs of

Shrewsbury and Chelmsford, I witnessed homophobia and racism in action for the first time, sometimes directed at the very students who were bringing prosperity to Leicester from abroad. Finding practical ways to help overseas students work their way around the Home Office rules, tackle racism from landlords, understand the Students' Union, and start to engage with it more regularly, are probably what got me elected as president after my final year of studies.

At just twenty years of age, I was suddenly responsible for forty-five staff members, shops, bars, cafés, gigs, parties, travel and insurance centres, as well as liaising with the polytechnic authorities. This gave me the confidence to apply for a range of jobs when I left. I chose HR as a consequence of spending some time in a tribunal, defending my decision to dismiss a member of the bar staff, whom I had caught red-handed, stealing cash from the till.

Thanks to this experience, my CV now stood out from the many other graduates applying for jobs. Against as many candidates as there are days of the year, I secured my first proper job as a trainee personnel officer at Wycombe District Council, who covered my costs of taking a college diploma in personnel management (which made up for the dire wages).

I happily moved between roles on rotation. Perhaps the best three months were in Time Study. For one week I had to follow a refuse lorry and record every pickup at every house, using a stopwatch to check how long it took them to pull the bin out, unload it and put it back. This data would be used later to draw up bonus schedules for the collectors. I filled in all the forms, worked out the averages, and proudly handed in my completed work to the Head of Work Study. He laughed out loud after just a few seconds reading the data. Apparently, all my figures were twice as long as they should have been, and I had been completely taken in by the refuse team! The only good thing I can say is there were no bins left outside on the road that day, there was no mess left behind, and the number of complaints from residents had fallen from an average of eleven to zero. Whilst making the mean average collection time per bin as high as possible, my crew had meticulously emptied each bin, taken it back to exactly where they found it rather than leaving it on the verge, and picked up any remaining litter.

Having completed my trainee role and my HR diploma, I found a personnel officer role in a commercial market research company in Oxford. My first task was to organise the graduate recruitment milk round, giving presentations along with free food and drink to final year students in the evening, and then running personality tests alongside interviews the following day, before travelling to the next university and repeating that for a month. The tests were 16PF (sixteen personality factors) and AH6 (Alice Heim cognitive reasoning ability). The American parent company had identified an ideal personality profile that had to be achieved for a candidate to be successful. After analysing all the data and reviewing all the interview notes I selected the top eleven candidates from around the country who fitted the profile. Then, being a rebellious type, I included one whose personality profile was the exact opposite of the parent company's diktat, to make up the required dozen. I'm still smiling today as I report that the first person to move from a trainee role into a full marketing research role, and later went on to be an outstanding regional director with a competitor, was my number twelve.

After a spell in a more senior role at another market research company in Ealing, I spotted my dream role advertised in *New Scientist*. Here was my chance to combine my love of science with a successful and growing pharmaceutical company, Glaxo Group Research, in Greenford. In my fourteen years there I was involved in two major mergers, undertook a big culture change project working alongside experts like Dave Ulrich and Lynda Gratton, learned how to lead progressively larger teams, and took part in some impressive development programmes at INSEAD, Duke Fuqua and London Business School. When you work in a large company, you have access to deep experts in their field and high performing teams made from the very best minds. It's a huge privilege. The downside was that I had more air miles than I could use, and a young family who needed more time and support.

After leaving Glaxo, I therefore turned down some bigger corporate roles, and swapped for a tiny biotech called RiboTargets. There I helped build a vibrant and productive culture, with some of the best scientists in their field. RiboTargets reversed into British Biotech and acquired Vernalis, adding Ionix and others over the years to come. As the company grew, we added some simple things, on a small budget, to keep everyone happy. They included a BBQ and outdoor seating, support for sports teams, and a decent rest room plus pool table, before they became popular all over the planet. My CEO had already beaten me to a proper Italian coffee machine, which was *the* place in the building to catch up on news.

After leaving Vernalis, and before becoming a consultant, I spent five years at the Medical Research Council, helping to change their pay and grading systems, so that the scientists and technicians were better rewarded for the amazing jobs they did. Thereafter, I spent three years at Wellcome Trust, where I established staff representative meetings, introduced mental health first aiders and made a series of improvements to the layout and use of the building, such as the introduction of a barista on the fifth floor. In both roles I worked with researchers in Africa and Asia, and introduced a new training programme for scientists to develop as managers, using an online suite specially commissioned from the Open University.

More recently I have worked as a consultant in human resources, organisation development and design, mostly supporting smaller companies, and I have enjoyed using my spare time to chair a charity called the Ideas Foundation, which works with young people from disadvantaged and ethnic minority backgrounds, helping them discover their creativity and grow in confidence. This followed periods as a non-executive trustee at Wysing Arts and time as chair of Herts Careers Service.

In summary, I'm a 'people director' best known for my creativity, with a focus on productivity and development. I have wide experience in business strategy, culture change, team leadership, mergers and acquisitions, in both private and public sectors, covering Europe, US, Africa and Asia. I've led major strategic reviews covering culture, information technology and research management, succession planning and talent retention; I've given presentations on the war for talent, culture change and life/work balance in both Europe and the States; I've coached senior board executives, managers and trainees, and mentored way too many people to count; and I've built, rebuilt, and learned how to motivate teams of HR and OD professionals, whilst keeping stakeholders and budget providers onside (mostly!).

The best HR folk have a mix of skills and competencies that include sales, statistics, communications, empathy, listening, interviewing, presenting, investigating, counselling, mediating and leading. Integrity, honesty, inclusion and the maintenance of dignity for all are their weapons of choice.

Much of the inspiration for this book has come from readers of my articles on LinkedIn, attendees of my presentations, and those who continue to ask me questions for my *Dear Ted* posts. If you don't find the answer to your question in this book, then come and find me on *LinkedIn*, my handle is UkTedSmith, and ask me there. I'll spend time with you (at no cost) discussing your issue, and then I will post a generic answer for others afterwards. And if you don't find me there, then you'll find me at festivals, live sports and gigs, travelling in my camper van or stopping off at the odd real ale festival.

ADHD

I used to associate ADHD with parents trying to find an excuse for their offspring to have extra support when at junior school, or more time in exams at senior school. I would shake my head and wonder why the kids were allowed sugary drinks containing tartrazine, and how they could always get away with such bad behaviour. How wrong was I?

Attention Deficit Hyperactivity Disorder is not a disease and it cannot be 'cured', but it is a disorder that can be treated effectively. ADHD comes in many forms, with varying levels of severity. The linking factor is that most people who are diagnosed have difficulty in concentrating on a subject or task, as well as having to deal with impulsiveness and periods of high levels of activity. It has been found through the use of MRI scanning that they have different structural properties and chemical balances in their brain, resulting in functional problems.

To prepare this chapter, I interviewed a nurse who is not only qualified to support people with ADHD, but also has the diagnosis herself.

Treatments come in the form of various types of medication, taken in assorted combinations, alongside therapeutic interventions. Counselling and coaching of techniques to reduce the impact of ADHD, also play an important part. As with so many medicines, pharmacological treatments often have unwelcome side effects, and a common one is appetite suppression. For Sue this has led to work colleagues wrongly assuming she is anorexic, which can be upsetting.

Sue only found out that she had ADHD when she was an adult. For most people it is picked up in childhood and treated from an early age, but this doesn't always happen. Some parents refuse to have their child referred for assessment (a process which looks at episodes in early toddler life, school, social life, sports and home settings), because they are worried about the stigma attached to the diagnosis. Other times it is because teachers or the local GP fail to recognise the signs. In such cases, a child will not then get the coaching and extra support they may need, and will often not reach their full potential as a consequence.

In discussing her life with ADHD, Sue talked me through an average day. Her disorder frustrates her because her symptoms get in the way of everyday life. All the time. She regularly gets locked out of the house or her car by forgetting her keys. She struggles with a trip to the supermarket, getting distracted by all the special offers and the regularity with which goods are moved around the store. She will arrive home with a random set of ingredients that won't make a meal, and will have to go back again. One day she set a personal record by having to make five separate trips to get what she needed. Meal planning doesn't happen and cooking often fails, so her diet can be somewhat hit and miss. Sue writes appointments in her diary, and then forgets to look at it. She knows she needs her medication, but forgets to order it. And she lives at either full speed, or dead stop, as a consequence of all these complicating factors.

When life is at full speed, and she is engaged with a subject, Sue is passionate, focused and productive. She describes these as her 'superwoman' moments. She's had some of her best ideas, made some wonderful breakthroughs and felt really good about life, recognising that she has something special to offer.

Sue likes to analyse and reflect, so much so that she says she can get stuck in her own thoughts. This leads to the dead-stop status, where she just needs to stand and stare at a wall (yes, quite literally), whilst she processes all the data whirring around in her head.

Sue is aware that she can become sensitive when challenged or criticised (RSD: Rejection Sensitive Dysphoria is worth a read via a search engine). This can be particularly difficult in a work setting, and it's here that the impact of ADHD can be profound.

Made to feel included and properly supported, Sue is one of the most productive people in the workforce, with a clarity and insight that goes way beyond the norm. Without the right support, her self-confidence and self-esteem plummets, and she becomes much less productive. Indeed, Sue can be sensitive to any push-back or challenge, and becomes angry, losing all focus of the objective in hand.

To be genuinely inclusive as employers, we need to spend time understanding what it is like to be one of the 3% of the population with ADHD, and we shouldn't assume that everyone who has this disorder is either aware that they have it, or that they are receiving the correct treatment. Equally, we should remember that people like Richard Branson and Will-I-Am have self-disclosed as having ADHD, and they haven't done too badly for themselves!

Taking everything into consideration, here are some tips for the line manager and HR business partner of someone diagnosed with ADHD:

- You need to read about and understand ADHD at a basic level.
- ADHD is a recognised disability and, as such, is a protected characteristic. If you are aware of a candidate with ADHD applying for a role, then you should take appropriate measures to accommodate any reasonable requests for the interview, or for the work environment if appointed or promoted.
- If the person is required to drive as a part of their role, it may be sensible to refer to Occupational Health for an assessment, and a reasonable adjustment might be the provision of an automatic car.
- Consider providing ongoing coaching support to give the ADHD person an outlet for their emotions, if they are triggered, and help with finding a way to be at their most productive.
- Provide a virtual 'time out' card that the person can use when needed to pause what they are doing and regroup.

- When devising away-days or team meetings, ensure there are proper breaks for the ADHD folk to pause and reflect. These breaks will also be loved by the introverts. Not everyone can withstand an 8 am start in a hotel away from home and a 10 pm finish without experiencing stress.
- When giving feedback of any kind remember the hypersensitivity and that you must set the feedback in context, not simply deliver it head-on. For example, don't mark-up a Word document and return it by email: talk it through instead, explaining the background to the issue and why it matters.
- Give feedback in a positive way and show the person a way forward. Negativity will usually backfire.
- If you can, offer a mobile phone number upfront and in advance. It is inevitable that someone in the workplace will say something inappropriate at some point; if they can phone you and get it out of their system, the sooner the better for productivity.
- Sometimes ADHD people just need space and time to themselves, and sometimes moods can fluctuate during a day. If you can recognise and accept this, things will go well.
- Avoid saying phrases like 'toughen up', 'stop being oversensitive', 'just concentrate on this for now' and 'have you had your meds today?'. Whilst you might mean well, these are likely to go down very badly indeed.
- Believe in them and trust them.
- Accept that there will be errors in their written work. Find a way to take the best bits and enhance them, rather than criticise and make fun of them.
- Accept that when they do something for the first time, they will feel vulnerable and far more sensitive than usual.

- If they become emotional about something, give them a chance to talk it through with you, and know that it will resolve with time.
- Understand that sometimes they won't be able to see through the fog of ADHD, and will need time to reflect and recover, before re-joining you and your team.

3

Appraisals

In my very first HR role, as a trainee, I was asked to rewrite the appraisal forms used by my company. At every subsequent organisation I worked at, people either wanted to change the forms or the system, all believing they could make it better. The truth is, an appraisal system is only as good as the managers who use it. Those who see it is as an inconvenience will want to find a way to complete the boxes and return the forms as quickly as possible, whereas effective leaders will already have discussed all the issues with each team member, as the year has progressed. The only way you can improve things is by providing training and development for your line managers in how to hold constructive conversations with their direct reports, where they actually listen to what is being said and take appropriate action.

If, as a line manager, you think less about appraisal, and more about how you can coach and lead your team, the better you will get at this process.

My advice is that you should spend your time and effort in training and developing your line managers, and not invest heavily in a new, 'better' software appraisal product until you have done so. And you should ensure that there are regular high-quality meetings between line managers and their direct reports that discuss their workload, their objectives, their training and any developmental needs, and that these are followed though.

4

Appraising the Appraisers

Some organisations have fixed calendar appraisals that link to pay review, others keep them separate, some prefer not to have a formal system at all, but best practice, as generally accepted, is that everyone should have a regular opportunity to review their work and their development. This includes senior line managers and board members.

The CEO should review each member of the exec team, and then the CEO should be appraised by the chair of the board. The chair also has the task of reviewing the work of the other board members, and the chair themselves is normally reviewed by the senior independent board member, who will sound out the views of the other board members, and the CEO, before their conversation.

In larger organisations, independent reviews of boards are often carried out on behalf of the chair by HR consultants, who also examine board effectiveness and diversity, ensuring that appropriate training is in place, and that members haven't overstayed their usefulness, and are sufficiently independent. Use of consulting support in this way removes the conflict of the chair reviewing the senior independent and vice versa.

Both charitable and commercial organisations have fallen foul of best practice and run into trouble, and it is often because relationships at the top have become too comfortable. Food for thought!

5

Autism

Having spoken to several people with autism, my central learning is that there truly is a wide range of types and levels of autism, the full spectrum as it is known. If, working in HR, you are asked to provide advice and support, do not assume that you know anything, unless in your previous life you have been a specialist in this field. Have a chat with the person, allowing plenty of time and, if possible, speak to their support worker. Find out exactly what their needs are, and what needs to be done to make the workplace more inclusive.

The following notes and tips are based on interviews with Mary, an autistic woman, carried out during lockdown. And there, immediately, was an issue. The government had just switched its advice from 'Stay At Home' to 'Stay Alert'. Just what does that mean to someone who needs clear instructions to understand what they are expected to do? Mary felt that 'Stay Alert' placed an impossible responsibility on her, especially when the virus could not be seen, heard, or tasted. She argued that the Government were setting her up to fail, and that it would now be her fault if things went wrong.

Mary explained that the lack of clear communication placed her on edge, and her lack of interaction with others during lockdown led to increased anxiety and tension, with limited opportunities to help her understand what the 'new normal' was.

Our first interview was delayed at the start, because Mary had just got an ice cream out of the freezer and was tucking in to it. She explained that her 'executive function' was non-existent. The day before she decided she needed a shower (something she is, in her own words, OCD about), moments before her support worker knocked on the door. The appointment was in her diary, but it didn't mean that she could make a decision about the order in which things should happen, or whether there was sufficient time between appointments.

Having got her to start talking about life with autism, Mary was distracted by an alert on Instagram, something she loves. When I got her attention again, she explained that she takes scores of photos and videos of herself, and uploads them to various social media sites. So much so that she gets blocked regularly, and occasionally is banned. Why am I giving this detail? Simply because it will give you an idea about the complexity of issues.

Mary recognises that she can be impossible to live or work with. She suffers episodes, the most frightening of which make her hate herself and feel unworthy. She has refused most medications that have been offered, on the grounds that their long-term use is still unknown, they could damage her, they pacify her, and they make her drowsy and want to sleep. Mary wants to be an engaged member of society, giving something back, so these side effects are unwelcome. She has accepted the help of support workers, and she was attending regular one-to-one therapy sessions until COVID-19 intervened and they had to be stopped.

Mary has to live with a sense of paranoia, which is common for many people diagnosed with autism. Her default position is to blame herself for anything that goes wrong, or doesn't work out well. This means that even constructive criticism can be misconstrued and often leads to a sleepless night or two as she tries to process the information. And if she sends an email about something that affects her and doesn't get a response, she will often catastrophise the issue, jumping straight to the conclusion that the person no longer likes her or wants her in their circle, or worse, that she is about to be dismissed. The fact that she is aware of these issues, and can talk about them with me, unfortunately doesn't mean that she can rationalise them in the moment, or control them.

In the work environment, if something is of real interest to Mary, she can develop what she calls a 'micro-focus' on the subject and can become highly productive. This has led to some excellent work, including research projects, curated displays, exhibitions and even shows.

Outside her job, Mary is used to being stared at by strangers while shopping or visiting friends. She swings from days when she would love a big badge proudly saying *I'm Autistic*, to days when she would prefer to be ignored and treated as 'normal', whatever that is. But being stared at in public is nothing compared to the abuse she has suffered, both mental and physical. Through the years people have taken advantage of her, ridiculed her, mocked her, taken pity on her, physically hurt her, and yet she has somehow managed to keep going, believing she needs to work towards a world where people with neuro-diverse backgrounds are welcome in society, and all the special things that are currently done become unnecessary.

Although I have stated above that everyone with autism is different, I still chose to ask Mary for some help with tips for HR teams and employers wanting to make someone like her feel more included and supported at work. Interestingly, she found it easier to talk about the negatives, leaving me to turn them around into positive tips.

- Double or treble the amount of time assigned to the initial induction in HR. Mary needs to start to build a relationship beyond that which occurred at interview, and know that she has someone she can trust and turn to if things get difficult, without everything having to land in the lap of her line manager. In this way she can keep a professional relationship with her boss, and avoid it getting too close to her personal issues, which will flare up from time to time.
- If you elect to use an external occupational health service, ensure that one person is assigned to work with her. It is immensely unproductive for Mary to have to keep going through

the process of relationship-building. A call centre approach requires extra care.

- Set clear expectations, and ensure that communications aren't ambiguous. If there are doubts, talk them through with Mary, rather than just emailing them to her. This applies as much to mundane things like rota changes as it does to policy changes.
- Avoid surprises. A sudden call, text or email out of the blue can cause concern and confusion, even paranoia.
- Don't patronise her because she appears to be slow, or appears not to hear something the first time. Mary will sometimes need extra time to process information, but it's not because she is thick – far from it. Instead, she is processing *every* eventuality, like a chess Grand Master, including scenarios you could not possibly conceive.
- Be prepared to halt her in mid-flow if she goes off at a tangent. Her mind moves in mysterious ways and sometimes needs to be steered back to the question in hand.
- Have a support system in place. If Mary has a personal issue, she needs to know who she can turn to. If not dealt with properly, then she can go downhill, in terms of her productivity, relatively quickly. Given that she can get into quite difficult personal problems, her support person also needs a supervisor (in the confidential sense of a coaching supervisor, so that the burden can be shared).
- Mental Health First Aiders should be briefed to immediately signpost someone like Mary straight to her support team, rather than assume they can step up to the mark. Their own training is not sufficient to help someone like Mary and they may do more harm than good.

Hopefully you will find that it is worth making these small investments. You will then benefit from having someone like Mary in your team, and the richness and insights that it brings, together with others recognising you as a truly inclusive employer.

Now to conclude with the most important take-home note. Think twice before reaching for the disciplinary code when someone like Mary misses an appointment. Remember that her executive function is nothing like that of others. She may have been distracted, a support worker may be helping her through an issue, or she might have got carried away in the moment, completing a piece of research and losing all track of time. If it is the latter reason, then be ready for something quite extraordinary to emerge.

6

Awards

Awards come in all shapes and sizes, from a simple thank you delivered privately, to receiving a gong at a ceremony, where all your sector peers have voted for you, or your idea.

Awards don't work for everyone, especially those who are introverted or have a preference to remain out of the limelight, but they can become fantastic tools for rewarding and motivating both individuals and teams.

When I was at the Medical Research Council, I uncovered a plethora of awards that the scientists and researchers could achieve, all provided by learned societies. If they invented a new technique, or developed an understanding of an area of science not previously known, they would receive an award at a ceremony and be lauded by their counterparts, right up to and including the honour of a Nobel Prize. Their support staff, however, got an invite to the champagne reception held the next day, and were thanked, but often that was it.

I debated this with my team and we launched the CEO Awards, to be given out to the best supporting team, or maybe a Lifetime Achievement Award for a long-serving technician. We came up with five titles in the first year, invited nominations, held a panel meeting with judges, and then invited the winners and runners-up to a ceremony to get their award and a professional photo of themselves receiving it from the CEO. We also presented everyone nominated with a certificate. The response was fantastic. It both lifted spirits and allowed people working behind the scenes to share airtime with their more celebrated leaders. When I transferred to work for the Wellcome Trust, I introduced a similar scheme for the facilities and HR staff, with some of the prizes donated by the partner contractors. Again, it had a positive impact on everyone, especially for the catering staff to be looked after and waited on by their director and managers. Easy to do, easy to replicate, with an undeniable impact on morale.

7

Bereavement

In the HR world we have to support people who lose a parent, child or close friend whilst they are working with us. Often, we are the first point of contact. And every time we are reminded that there is no book, or process, or procedure to follow, because everyone responds differently.

When I was fourteen, my father died of a second heart attack. I jumped into action, taking responsibility for my mum and younger sister, phoning the bank (creating a nightmare for my mum who couldn't take any cash out for weeks), talking to relatives and generally trying to organise everything. No tears, just head down and sort this out. Back at school the next day, literally.

A few years ago, my mother died. I jumped into action, made arrangements, registered the death, sorted the funeral and the wake, had a nightmare with Lloyds (her will was in their safe, but we needed a copy of the will to access the safe!) and generally organised everything. No tears, just head down and sort this out. Back in the office the next day, literally.

A week after my mum died, our fourteen-year-old Labrador died. I was useless. I couldn't work out what to do, or understand why I felt so useless. Lots of tears. I needed time off work to get myself together. I then saw *Field of Dreams* (the version with Kevin Costner), and again erupted in floods of tears, as I started grieving for my dad at long last.

From my personal experience I can tell you there's no logic or reason behind how and when people will be affected by bereavement, and certainly no way an HR policy manual can account for the best way to support someone.

When I was a trainee in local government, I remember an elderly colleague trying to explain to a newly bereaved carpenter that the death of his aunt was not an excuse to have a day off, but for a parent or child the scheme would allow up to two days at the management's discretion. The irony was that the aunt in question had been the guardian of this man since he was three years old. But the rules said no, and no it was. He had to take annual leave. The carpenter carried a grudge against HR and the council for many years after that. It really troubled me at the time.

Much later, when I was working for a small biotechnology company, I was approached by one of the team whose mother was unwell in eastern Europe. After a chat to the CEO, not only did we give the employee a week off, but we covered the cost of flights. No payback was wanted or expected, but it's amazing how news like that travelled around the team. Loyalty is built through such actions. So, what can we do in HR?

The first thing, as highlighted above, is not to reach for the manual or staff handbook. Instead it's to find a private space and start by just listening. Give the person a chance to talk about their loved one (human or animal, it matters not), to talk about how unjust the world is, or in some cases just to resolve practical questions, because they might well be in admin mode, as I was as a child. Beware of any questions that relate to pensions or money, however, and don't make promises that you can't keep. Carefully note down the questions, and then get back to them as soon as you know the answers, keeping them up to date if the pensions provider needs extra time, for example.

Remember that their head could well be spinning, they might not be sleeping well, so don't assume they are taking in everything you're saying, and send them an email soon after your chat, just to confirm what you have heard them say, where they can get help, and what the organisation can offer. Don't force them to go home (I've seen that go down really badly), since the most useful thing for them right now might be the distraction of work, or the ability to use the company computer and telephones, and know they have people around them for support as needed.

Ask them for permission to share the news with other members of the team. Some people find this difficult and you'll be doing them a favour, but if they refuse, then keep everything confidential (albeit you need to explain that their line manager should be made aware).

Think creatively about how the team can help them the most. If they have only just heard and come straight to HR, one option might be to find a volunteer to drive them to wherever they need to go. You don't want them having an accident driving themselves. On the practical side, it might be that you research and find some useful fact sheets for them: what to do in the case of a death; registering a death; insurance and pensions. Everything is out there on the internet, but your cool head might find them faster than their spinning head.

If your employee becomes a single parent, can you provide practical support in finding childcare solutions that will allow him or her back to work when the time is right? Is some counselling going to be helpful? Does a member of their team need to step up and take on some additional responsibilities whilst they sort things out?

Reassure them that they can take the time they need to sort things out. For example, it's not possible to arrange a funeral until the postmortem is completed, and the coroner has given their opinion. Often that can't happen until the GP has been found and they have opined, or the registrar has completed their paperwork, all of which can be postponed by public holidays, etc. And that's before we even talk about solicitors and probate, inheritance tax or clearing and selling a house.

Try not to jump to conclusions, listen empathetically and fight their corner *with* them, and you'll be remembered for a long time, as well as knowing that you have made a real difference.

8

Blind or Visually Impaired

Whilst working at the Wellcome Trust as Director of People and Places, I had the privilege to work with Aidan Kiely, who had been born blind. Towards the end of our time working together I had a long chat with him about his life and what sighted people could learn from him. Some of his answers made me think and act quite differently thereafter. I wrote this section, but Aidan has edited it, adding some quotes and changing the emphasis of some parts.

Due to a recessive family gene, Aidan was born completely blind, with no notion of dark, light or colour. His blindness was a complete surprise to his family, and it has been a learning curve ever since. Aidan has always been mature beyond his years and is very much at ease with his blindness, explaining, 'I'm really pleased that my sister was born sighted and that this happened to me, because for me it has opened as many doors as it has closed, and I really do feel strongly about that.'

Aidan attended a specialist primary school, so it wasn't until he went to secondary school that he was confronted with his difference to others. It clearly didn't get in his way, as his intellect and desire to learn took him through school and up to Cambridge university, where he completed his MA, before taking an MSc at Manchester. Aidan worked in the NHS and wider healthcare sector in various project roles before joining me at Wellcome, where he played a key role in continuous improvement, alongside opening the eyes of the Diversity and Inclusion team. Aidan is one of those few people in life who constantly inspire me. His positive attitude to life is amazing, and he has also given a great deal of his time to supporting and mentoring others.

One of my early hang-ups was using phrases such as 'What is your vision for the project' or 'Can you see where this is going' in front of Aidan. Like the word 'insight' above, they are commonplace terms, and it's easy to use them without thinking. Aidan realised I was stumbling over these words and started to use them deliberately in his own vocabulary, to help put me at ease. He always encourages people to chat to him as normally as they can and disregard words like 'see', 'look' and 'vision'. It took me a while, but it was worth it when I got there.

So, what is it like being blind? Can we sighted folk gain an insight? That's probably impossible. But let's give it a go.

When sighted people reference things like a large building or an airplane (objects that are too large for him to touch), Aidan explains that he has the ability to conceive such concepts by continually learning and adding to his vocabulary, and understanding comparisons like small and large and wide versus narrow. He learned about shapes at primary school through tactile objects, and these help him to complete the 3D jigsaw puzzle in his mind. When it comes to 'watching' a movie, Aidan says, 'It's not just about looking at the screen, it's also about the atmosphere that the director creates, the dialogue between the actors, the events that occur and the emotions evoked, hence to watch a movie is actually to experience a movie.'

The concept of colour is through learned understanding. He tells me that different colours evoke different responses, feelings and experiences in people and he has learned to feel these for himself. Red for excitement or anger, the calming nature of blue and the environmental credentials of green. By learning the differences that sighted people express about colours, he can get a feel for them, and play a full part in conversations, something he has always worked on.

Where Aidan has a distinct advantage over others is in an interview. He has no clue about the colour of an interviewee's skin, their choice of clothes, their hair colour, tattoos or piercings. And so instead he concentrates on what they say. And he's had some funny moments where he admits he has made an assumption based on the candidate's name or accent, only to discover later they were from a quite different ethnic background to his first guess.

Other funny moments include answering someone in the street whom he thought was asking how he was, only to discover they were talking to their mobile phone, and realising too late that he had asked a very small child on a train if he knew which station they had just passed. The child ended up getting help from their mother and grandmother, so it became a great opportunity to meet a new family!

Discrimination, as Aidan says, is a broad term with different meanings for different people. Thankfully, direct discrimination is a rare event for him, but it pops up at odd times. He can't, for example, vote in secret. Someone has to complete the ballot form for him.

After some poor experiences, the choice of companies that he works with is now predicated on how helpful they are at discussing his needs and accommodations that can be made before he starts. Those accommodations are actually quite simple: a laptop with software that converts text to audio; remembering to give Aidan advance copies of meeting slides so he can convert them to audio before attending; a fixed (not hot) desk that he can get to know; time with a colleague to learn routes to places in the building (toilets, canteen, tea station, reception, lifts, etc.); a tailored fire-evacuation plan; and a chat with the facilities team not to create new trip hazards without first alerting Aidan (like leaving a *This Floor is Wet* sign at the top of the stairs).

Aidan's top tips for sighted people to be aware of when meeting someone who is blind are:

- Don't force people to cross roads that they don't want to cross! Ask if they want help, and listen to the answer.
- Don't help out by showing a blind person a short cut, as it will take them away from their known route, and could leave them

disorientated. Routes are carefully planned and part of their established routine.

- Don't make a big fuss of them in a social context. There's nothing more embarrassing than being announced to a room full of strangers when you just want to blend in.
- Be as discrete as you can when helping. This is not a moment for you to try and win an award for being a great citizen; you can help best by being quietly respectful, and not by telling everyone at the table that you're going to help Aidan, who now has soup on his shirt!
- When talking to a blind person that you know, start by saying who you are. Just because they are blind or impaired doesn't mean that they can automatically recognise your voice straight off. There is no proof that blind people have superpowers with their hearing, in the same way that deaf people don't have X-ray vision to compensate.
- Think of the impact of what you are about to do. For example, Aidan was crossing a road when someone shouted at him to 'watch out', but didn't say what for. Aidan froze on the spot, thinking he was about to hit something, but he would have been better advised to keep walking and therefore avoid the speeding police car heading towards him (spoiler alert: he survived that one)!
- Trim trees and bushes and take care with other objects that overhang pavements. Whilst a white stick helps find obstacles on the floor, it doesn't save Aidan's forehead from being hit by branches, estate agents' signs and scaffolding.
- Remember that people with impaired vision or blindness have good and bad days. If you offer to help and get a gruff response, don't let it put you off offering help in the future. They might just have had a crappy day and need their own space.

- If you get in the way of someone with a white cane, don't scream or shout or make sudden or erratic movements. Usually the best thing to do is stand still and allow the person to go around you. They probably have their regular route and will be used to occasional new things getting in the way, whether human, animal or mineral.
- If you see someone with a white cane walking very slowly, or moving in a circle, do approach them. The chances are they are out of their routine, or are in a new area, and need help. If you can get them to a landmark of their choosing, they can then re-orientate and get back on their way.
- Watch out for someone needing help on a day of extremes. Remember that a routine path can seem strange if the weather has taken away the temperature changes, the breeze or the sounds that a blind person is expecting and using for navigation. As an example, Aidan got 'lost' on his way to the restaurant inside the building because the fridge he was used to turning right at had been turned off. The way the space around you works is different if you cannot rely on sight.

Regarding the offers of help that Aidan gets, he points out that the most important thing for him is to feel in control. If he has been consulted and then consented to walk with aid, knowing where he is going, or which road he is crossing, then everything is fine. What he doesn't want is impulsive acts of unwanted 'help' that can set him back.

I asked Aidan about his favourite spaces (a term he uses to describe the places that he visits). His first was his house, a familiar place where he knows where things are, where he can relax with his family and live his life without any pressures. His second was a surprise for me: an open field in the countryside. Although it's a space where he needs to be guided, here he can feel the wind, hear the trees and the birds, he can find peace and calm and appreciate nature.

I also asked about the questions that make Aidan cringe. So, take my tip and steer clear of asking about his sex life: he has just as much trouble and hassle as the rest of us, thank you very much! As Aidan says, 'nothing is insurmountable', proving that he has a fine sense of humour.

And finally, if soup is his nemesis (if you are designing a menu for a company banquet, please do think about this), what is his favourite food? No hesitation: fish 'n' chips. Aidan and I have more in common than we realised.

Bureaucracy

Bureaucracy is easiest to spot when you first arrive at a new organisation, but if you've been there a while, ask new recruits to highlight those things that drive them round the bend whilst they are still finding their way around. I regularly find time to speak to people a month or so after they have started, to hear how they are getting on, find out what they like and what is getting in the way of them doing a great job. I've learned so much by this process, and all it has cost me is a few coffees and teas. If you don't understand why a form has to be filled in, or struggle with a convoluted process to achieve an action, just ask. Be persistent and pursue the issue back to its origins. A lot of the most bureaucratic processes were put in place years previously to counter a problem relevant at that time. If life has moved on but no one has had the courage to challenge the process, now is your moment. And driving out bureaucracy will make you many friends.

Board Members

If you're in a smaller, or medium-sized organisation, there is a chance you will get to meet some of your NEDs (non-executive directors). This might be at a remuneration committee meeting or similar, or at an AGM. It matters not when; remember these people have chosen to support the organisation, and that they lead their own lives outside work. Find an excuse to chat, to find out a bit more about them, and start building a relationship.

A great way I have found is to look up their profiles and understand why they are in their current position. What in their history led to their current status? Then I find a link to something I am trying to achieve at work and simply ask for their advice. I have never been turned away. Every time I have received something back: a chance for a separate chat over coffee; a flurry of emails or phone calls; even the opportunity to visit them at their main place of work and meet their HR people.

By building a relationship with one or more of your NEDs (clearly it is good to at least do this with your RemCo Chair), you can then seek support and help in the future, maybe offer something back (I have helped with a child's CV for example, although I try to avoid giving work experience to every relation of every NED), and, most importantly, lobby them in advance of board meetings where my ideas for change are being presented.

Although I use the word 'lobby', the best way if you have some time in hand, is to ask for their advice way before you take the paper to your exec, let alone the board. That way you will benefit from their knowledge, as well as have them on your side when the moment arrives.

In my experience, if you put something that is well thought through to a board, you will get usually get a favourable reception plus their personal opinions. Every NED believes they are the best people manager they know, so take some of the advice with a pinch of salt, but enjoy harnessing their expertise and enthusiasm to get things done.

Remember also that these people may be able to help you find a new job in the future, as well as provide references, so make sure there is good coffee and cake available at your next RemCo Meeting!

11

Budgeting

The biggest mistake you can make as a new head of a Human Resources function is to accept the old budget without question and try to work with it for the following year. Once you accept that, you will end up in an endless cycle, which effectively restricts you to fighting for an inflationary increase well into the future.

The simple truth is that the HR function is often seen as an expense by the head of finance: something to be tolerated, but not invested in. That is, unless there is a clear return on investment in any proposed project or change. (Often this pops up when a new HR system is being proposed, and the finance team assume that the costs of implementation will be offset by reduced HR running costs in the future.)

Always go back to basics when preparing a budget, and build from the bottom up. This means finding out when the budget cycle occurs and putting in the effort well ahead of time. What do you need operationally to provide a strong, basic service? What could you invest in to reduce your workload and give your team to provide advice and support in the key areas that impact productivity (e.g. outsourcing some of the repetitive functions of recruitment)?

Invest some time getting to know your finance team business partner, or in a smaller company, the CFO. They can help you with your budgeting, and will make things easier for you if they can feel the benefit of your presence within their own team.

12

Cancer

If you have a company handbook that has rules and procedures for handling sickness absence, please start by explaining to the line manager that it is utterly irrelevant when someone tells you they need to be treated for cancer. The same applies to a parent of a child, or the partner of a team member and your absence policy: it is irrelevant. Whilst it is increasingly the case that cancer can be treated and kept at bay, often for the rest of someone's working life, being told that you or a close member of the family has cancer creates all sorts of anxiety, stress, lost sleep and often mental ill health. Everyone has their own way of coping, and they need appropriate support and space, not a rule book that states how many days they can take off before their pay is stopped, or disciplinary action commences.

You would think that a person who has been told they have cancer and needs a lengthy course of treatment would be the most impacted, but I have often found it is the employees who are parents and partners who struggle the most, especially in the early days. The worst period is right at the beginning, awaiting results. They are distracted and unable to concentrate, often not wanting to talk about it on the off-chance that the news from the biopsy/scan/blood test is not good. They are hurting, worrying, sometimes overthinking what will happen. Were they responsible, what more can they do, what happens if...

I have witnessed a range of reactions once the news is given. The most common is a stoic response, along the lines of 'This won't beat me. I'm going to carry on as normal.' This is either accompanied by a request that no one in the work environment be told, or the exact opposite, that everyone is told and regularly updated. The former can be quite tricky. At some point people in the team become curious about the amount of time off work the person is taking, why they 'aren't their normal selves', or similar questions that arise. You need an agreed plan to deal with this, and you will *always* need the line manager to be involved.

Although common, not everyone presents with the British stiff upper lip. There will be a small number who are derailed by the news and need extra support and help right from the beginning. There is no defined way to help in such circumstances, but the best is usually to ask good friends to provide help until family members can free-up time. This is where I have found Macmillan Cancer Support to be invaluable. They run a 24/7 phone helpline in the UK, staffed by specialist nurses and counsellors with experience of every type of issue that you will face, and they give tremendously practical and helpful advice. At least 25% of my royalties for this book will go to them.

The reality of the impact that a course of chemotherapy and/or radiotherapy has on an individual often only hits home a month or so in. Different cancers have different regimes, and different consultants have different preferred courses of treatment, but whilst many find that the first trips for treatment aren't as bad as they expected, the treatment regime eventually wears them down. The body starts to react to the treatment, and side effects such as nausea, bloating and hair loss lead to physical and mental fatigue. This is where the rule book has to be disregarded. A parent will need to accompany their child to the hospital and be with them whilst they recover; a stoic patient who is proud of taking a day for treatment and then returning to work may realise that they need a few extra days, or longer, before they can get back into work. And if you start telling them they only have a few days of parental leave left, or their sick pay is about to expire, then you are piling further stress and concern on top of a person already at the end of their tether, so just don't!

Look after someone when they have to deal with an issue like this, and they will repay you with their loyalty for years to come afterwards, and their work colleagues will do the same.

A well-meaning mistake made by some line managers is to tell someone they can have as much time off as they want, and then find a replacement for them. This might well be what is needed in some cases, but it requires careful discussion and reassurance. The last thing you want to do is to add to their pressure by putting a doubt in their mind about whether or not they will have a job to return to. If you do have to take this path, ensure that all the announcements make it clear this is an interim arrangement.

Some people have a treatment regime that impacts their immune system in such a way that, although they want to come back into the workplace, their consultant will be advising them against it, for fear they will catch an illness on the way into, or at, work. At this point the required absence can be for three or four months or more, and yet the person may want to keep busy and in touch. Being flexible and working with their wishes is key. In some cases, providing a laptop and keeping email and video-conference systems open is appropriate, offering the person a welcome distraction; in other cases agreeing an out-of-office message and setting that on the email system for the period can be the better solution.

Keeping in touch is critical. A text message or phone call, a letter with the latest news from work, an invitation for a Zoom or Skype, or to come in, or to meet at (or near) their home, should be made by whoever has taken the link role (often the line manager, sometimes the HR person, other times a close work colleague).

Once the treatment is concluded and the consultant or GP has given approval for a return to work, you need to think through the best approach with their line manager. Consider: the first day, meeting them outside the workplace and walking in with them; briefing them on changes in the workplace and agreeing appropriate flexible workload; a phased return, part-time building up to full-time; avoiding rush-hour travel; how to handle a full mail inbox; what to say to colleagues and clients on return; any special dietary or health needs; and sorting out a pay rise if they have missed a pay review.

A good friend who has just completed a course of chemo, and has recently returned to work has these additional suggestions, in her own words:

- Clear lines of communication must be kept open between the HRBP and the person at all times. If you are going to be away, let them know who is providing cover. People being treated for cancer will have good days and bad days, so, if they contact you with a query, be aware that it will probably be on a good day and they may not be able to contact you on another day, if treatment is difficult for them. Be patient with them and give them plenty of time to respond.

- If you need to send any important information to the employee, for example, regarding changes to salary, do not do this just as you are leaving the office on a Thursday evening for a long weekend! The person may want clarification and someone to discuss it with. If you are not there to talk to, this will provide added stress.

- If someone gives you an estimate of when you can expect them back at work, an estimate is all it is. Contact them a week before they are due to return and check in with them, extending sick pay arrangements as needed.

- Transitioning back to full-time employment after a long time away is difficult. It's actually much more difficult than leaving to go off sick. If your employee has had cancer, this might be the most traumatic thing they have ever dealt with in their lives.

- Cancer changes you on every conceivable level and the treatment dulls you down and can often cause chemo-brain. Be flexible with the amount of time they need on a phased return.

Confidence will be low, and they may even be terrified that they can't come back and work at 100% capacity. Chemo-brain can last for up to two years, causing forgetfulness, confusion and anxiety in the workplace. Be flexible and let them know they are still supported when they return to work.

- As an HRBP, stay in touch with the person's line manager after they return to work. There are no hard and fast rules for best practice when it comes to cancer. Everyone is different, but it would be useful for managers to have flexible guidelines to work with alongside their common sense and compassion. Ensure the manager is aware that the employee may not be at 100% with their working capacity, so that they can quietly inform others not to come to your desk to demand you do some work for them in your first hour back in the office!

13

Career Changes

Not everyone can sustain a role in Human Resources forever, and given that a working life can span anything up to fifty years, then a change in career is either something you will consider at some point, or something you will discuss with the people you mentor, who themselves might be looking to move on.

For someone who's worked in Human Resources, Training or Organisational Development, it's probably easier than they realise to change to another career. A firm understanding of CVs, an excellent telephone manner, the ability to talk to people in informal meetings and formal interviews, inside knowledge of how businesses work, a well-practiced sales patter: it's a pretty good start.

Think about what motivates and interests you (or your mentee if helping someone else). That should be the same for anyone switching career. If you are going to make a change, it might as well be into something that you're going to enjoy. If you can make your hobby your work, time will fly by. Think about the things that you love to be involved in, the hobbies, sports or other pastimes you engage with. Think about the compliments that people have paid you in the past. Is there something that ties them all together?

If you had a million pounds and could only spend it on a charity, what would that be and why? Questions like this get you thinking. Is there a training course or a development programme that you have always wanted to go on? If there is, have a chat to the head of department at the university that runs the most interesting courses. They would love to speak to a potential mature student of their course.

Once you start to form an idea, and it might need help from your mentors to see the wood for the trees, then research the area. Talk to other friends already in the field. Get in touch with the talent acquisition heads of organisations in that sector. Offer to buy them a coffee and chat through entry routes and possibilities. You'll learn a lot and, at the very worst, make new contacts.

Have a look at charities specialising in the field and/or colleges. Offer them voluntary support, maybe as a trustee or non-exec board member, again growing your contacts. If you can take the financial hit, then maybe negotiate with your current employer a four-day week, to give you extra time to make all these connections and attend interviews, or even to undertake part-time study for your new career.

In other words, try to make it a fun process and leave no stone unturned. I've seen a very successful recruiter retrain as a coach, an HRBP as a teacher, a trainer as a psychologist, and even one as a garden designer! I've also seen some excellent HR people take a course, such as an MBA, and enter general management roles, taking on quite different responsibilities, and, in one case, becoming CEO of a small company.

14

CEO

Working in Human Resources you often learn about a new CEO before announcements are made, especially when you work for a company listed in the markets, where the data can be share-price sensitive. If you're in a senior HR role you may well be asked to get involved with the work of the Remuneration Committee, or the Nominations Committee, as the package of pay and benefits is put together, possibly including relocation options. In the case of a CEO moving to the area it may be sensible to contract with a specialist agency who can help your new boss find a suitable house, consider schooling issues, etc. It's a time-consuming exercise and best left to the experts; remember that this might not be something you normally provide, but can be justified on the grounds of productivity: you want your new CEO up and running as quickly as possible.

Most new CEOs will meet their board non-execs well before they start, and they will usually meet the CFO and a few other execs in confidence, as a part of the selection process. If you can, grab a chance for an early chat and see what her preference is for induction. She might want a structured set of meetings, an all-hands town hall meeting, or she might prefer to walk around and meet people. Don't assume there is a specific approach and be ready to be flexible.

This will also be a good excuse to work closely with the EA or PA that will be working with the CEO. Remember that they might be quite nervous about a new boss (even if they don't show it) and will need some reassurance, and an excuse for an early meeting to discuss things like diary and email support.

To be most helpful and get a new CEO up to speed as quickly as possible, it is essential to try to understand the world from her perspective. When she's out of the office, go and sit in her seat and think through the issues she is dealing with. Talk regularly to her EA/PA and other directors, and keep on top of all that is going on, especially in the first hundred days.

After the initial settling-in period, have a chat with her to understand what she wants to achieve, and what she believes the blockers are. See if you can agree a plan of action, be ready to change your own ways of working to align with the new style she will bring, and work positively for her success. If she succeeds, so will the organisation, and that will probably include some kind of restructuring or re-organisation; remember that few CEOs are ever asked to come in and hold the place steady by the board!

Joining an organisation and working with an established CEO can be another kettle of fish entirely, especially if you report through another exec (e.g. the COO). You'll need to find opportunities to talk to them about ideas, sometimes seeding a thought and then following up at the next meeting. Again, I've always found that an important relationship to create and build on is with the EA/PA to the CEO. It's well worth taking them to coffee or lunch, chatting about all sorts of things, listening to what they say. Many times, you realise they could have done a much bigger job if they had chosen to, but they like the role they are in. As your relationship develops you can ask questions like 'Do you think [CEO name] would be interested in XYZ?' or talk to them about something that the CEO needs to do more, or less, of. They may find a moment and deliver the message for you. If you have spent time listening well, you may be able to change systems or processes for the benefit of the EA/PA. All these little things will lead to you getting into the CEO's diary when no one else can, so it's a good investment.

When you are in a new role and you're talking to an established CEO about potential changes, be thoughtful. They may well lend their energy and support to the very element you want to replace. Ask their opinion of the matter at hand, raise questions about it, suggest some alternatives, and let them take the lead. If they ask you to do something, then they will want to support it and see it through to conclusion. If you seeded the idea and they are now claiming as their own, go with the flow: at least you will make your desired change, and you can even include it on your CV as an accomplishment! Hopefully, you will have the opportunity to work with a smart CEO who is people orientated at some point in your career.

15

Change

Whilst working in HR I've been involved in restructures, mergers, multiple redundancies, new CEOs, new policies and new ways of working, to name just a few of the types of change that take place. The common link is that the HR team is expected to be there to offer calm advice and support, to uphold other people's perception of fairness and, in the big change programmes, to maintain dignity for those leaving, and continued motivation for those staying, all within the boundaries set by employment and case law.

Academics have studied change, and you will regularly see a smooth U-shaped curve (search for Kubler-Ross Change Curve) which is labelled with the progress made through a period of change. In the case of something like a restructuring, or merger, you will see a drop in productivity as people experience shock and denial, before getting frustrated and even depressed with the change that they are experiencing. Having reached rock bottom, the academics argue that most people then start to experiment and try out new things and, if they aren't made redundant or demoted by the change program, they will start to integrate with the new structure and processes, eventually being even more productive than before. Hence the smooth U-shaped curve which goes down and then back up. Well, that's the theory.

In real life, there is no such thing as a smooth transition. A rough approximation of my curve through a major merger was as follows: initial excitement at the opportunity as an HR guy to learn loads; then a dip with the realization of how much work was to follow; a further dip as projects I was passionate about were shelved; a leap up again when an exec told me how great I was and not to have any concerns, he'd look after me; a massive dip when he didn't get the job at his level of the re-structure; another big dip into the abyss as I learned that I had to fill in a load of forms and be interrogated by a bunch of re-engineering special-ists to get my own job back; an uptick when the new boss told me I was the chosen one; and back down when I was told I would have to relocate countries to make it work. And that is just a small part of my personal journey: as an HRD I was also carrying the ups and downs of so many people that I had worked with for so many years. It was exhausting, it was bumpy, and we never returned to the original productivity levels. Instead of a smooth U-shaped curve, we had the equivalent of a full set of waves, as if at sea in a small boat on a stormy day.

Everyone has their own unique curve, linked to personality and their perception of the impact on them and their colleagues. Some people have a more laid-back and relaxed view of life, but even they might be hiding concern and worry deep down inside, so everyone has to be cared for in an appropriate way.

The key is to ensure regular, open and honest communications about what is happening, that recognise that people may be at different points on their curve. So, for example, the gleeful announcement of a new divisional director being appointed during a merger will never go down well, because there will always be a group of people who were hoping that the other candidate got the role.

Rumours cause untold worries and concerns. They spin out of con-trol, they spread fast, and they are often started by people trying to get some information. They can therefore be dealt with by regular updates, sometimes brought forward specifically to deal with a rumour that is causing hurt. And that does not mean waiting for the Head of Com-munications and CEO to agree a text that says nothing, it means telling people in the moment what is actually happening. Sometimes it even means saying 'We are awaiting the outcome of a management meeting which takes place at noon tomorrow, and until then everything is just rumour.'

Change also impacts the HR team, and we don't often have an HR for HR, so we need to look after ourselves. We need to trust our own team, share confidential information, and make the communications twice as regular as for everyone else, so that the HR team can answer questions coming in. We need to support each other, maybe buddying up, and sometimes bring in specialist external support. When we were making large numbers of people redundant following the merger between Glaxo and Wellcome, we used to book time slots in our diaries where the HR team could go and just chat with each other about what had happened, sometimes over a wine or a beer.

What else can we do as HR professionals? At a time of great change, we need to be the ones who can hold our senior directors' feet to the fire, keep them honest, remind them when they are not walking the talk, encourage them to keep communicating and tell them when they are wearing no clothes. Equally, we need to be there for them, with empathy and support, when they are feeling low, exhausted or both. Who else will do these things at times of stress if not us?

At a more local and practical level we can also ensure that we have Wellbeing Champions in each division or department, who ensure the provision of appropriate resources and support for people as they go through the change. A good EAR (Employee Advisory Resource) scheme can provide an external independent outlet for people, and the better ones will provide face-to-face counselling. I've also seen therapies like neck and shoulder, or Indian head massages, take off at times of change. Some of these things will need a small budget, but if relieves stress and helps people become more productive, then surely it is worth the small additional cost?

16

Children

Many of my mentees have debated the timing of bringing up a family with me, and how it will affect their career. My advice has always been the same: if you have the courage to ask my views, then it's clear that starting a family is something you would love to do, and are actively considering, so go for it! There is always the possibility of a promotion, or interesting project, on the horizon, but there is also a time when your (or your partner's) biological clock may get in the way. For me, when I think about all the things I have achieved in my life, it's my two sons that give me the greatest sense of pride. Don't leave it too late if a family is what you want; a good employer will always support you, and a bad one isn't worth staying with.

17

Clothes and Uniforms

How can you make lasting decisions about an organisation if you don't understand it?

When I was asked to take on the role of representing facilities at exec level, my knowledge of the division and all that it encompassed was low. Aside from being a user of the services, I had little understanding of the size, complexity and, more importantly, the skills and experience of the people working in it.

For my facilities induction, I was briefed by the senior line managers and told about the standards they adhered to, their budgetary challenges and their objectives. Other users told me that whilst most things were great, some things needed to change. I needed to find out more than this before making decisions about policy and budgets.

I therefore booked a string of days in my diary over several months and approached the senior managers with the simple request that I spend at least a few days with each of their facilities teams, working with them. In other words, cleaning a window, rather than supervising it.

I wore the uniform of a security officer for a week (including a night shift), covering all the aspects of the role such as patrolling, recording incidents, replacing lost passes, chasing naughty kids, and helping an old man find shelter. I spent time as a trainee *Chef de Tournant*, meaning I learned how to sharpen and use a knife properly, prepared several hundred starters and cleaned some pans, before serving other employees. I cleaned toilets, kitchens, windows, floors and mirrors (well, I only smeared them, apparently), and I went up onto the roof in a harness to check the automatic wash system. I put on a red polo shirt and joined the site maintenance team and worked in the engineering group, maintaining air chiller units, replacing the hinges on a set of doors and attending desk repairs and alterations. I worked on reception and put phone calls through to the wrong people; I collected bins as a refuse collector; and I ordered stationery and more in the management offices, and was even allowed to use a photocopier and binder unsupervised.

I learned an enormous amount, not just about the operation, but about the people, how they were managed, where the issues lay, and I also learned a lot about human behaviour.

If you spend a day with a team it runs through a pattern. At the start, colleagues tend to be nervous. They are overly respectful and apologise when asking you to do things (like clearing up wee in a women's cubicle, which were far messier than the men's cubicles, by the way). As the day moves on, the banter starts up (unless you're with the engineers, in which case it starts before you have managed to sign all the risk assessment forms). Then it gets interesting, and by the end you realise you have a list of issues that really do need to be sorted out: ideas for saving the environment, saving money and enhancing the service. Additionally, you have your own ideas about which of the supervisors is a must-keep, and those that would benefit from some personal development.

You also know more about the lives of the people you are working with, the sacrifices they make for their loved ones, their illnesses, their pleasure that they now get at least the Real London Living Wage rather than the Government's watered-down version, and the reality of trying to get to work at 4 am on a slow night bus service.

Each of these short placements opened my eyes to the very different groups of people working in all these areas. I got to know people, their hopes and aspirations. I chatted to one person who was now a cleaner, but had previously been a financial controller. They didn't want anyone to know this, as they had chosen to make a complete change when coming to Britain. I worked alongside an ex-Olympic cyclist, who didn't want anyone to know because she was shy. I met a supervisor of a cleaning team who had such a phenomenal understanding of every detail of every job assignment, and the skills of every member of her team, that I encouraged her to think bigger (but she was content in her role). I also worked with people who were clever beyond their own understanding, who could find ways to make a job go faster or slower depending on the bonus scheme they were on, who could manipulate their supervisors with ease, and who loved the sport of it all!

I had the pleasure of encouraging some of the exceptional people that I met to take the next steps and develop their careers. I've always enjoyed doing this with HR assistants and administrators, seeing them progress into senior roles that they didn't believe were possible.

Not only have I found this to be powerful in offices and museums, but I've also had the chance to spend time in biology and chemistry labs, with research teams, with procurement and finance teams. Although I won't claim to understand everything they were trying to explain, I emerged with at least a better idea about their work. That made it even more fun when recruiting and being able to chat with meaning about specific bits of research kit!

The biggest shock, however, was the sheer number of people who looked through me when I was wearing a uniform. My normal attire in one office was chinos and an open-neck shirt. As soon as I wore a suit and tie, and stood near the doorway as a security officer, I was no longer Ted from HR, but Mr Security Officer. I would greet people that I knew and had worked with as they entered the building with a cheery 'Good morning', and either be ignored, or glanced at, with no acknowledgement. Several looked straight through me. A few muttered 'Good morning' back to me.

After my first day of this, I got so annoyed that I kept a tally on day two. I stopped at a hundred. Thirty-nine ignored my greeting altogether, forty-seven answered or muttered something back, six engaged with me and eight recognised me (of which only two asked what the heck I was doing dressed as a security officer!).

I had a similar experience as a receptionist (again, wearing a suit and tie). In a cleaner's uniform it was marginally worse, with people deliberately changing direction to avoid me and my cart, and wearing the obvious fear on their faces of having to acknowledge my existence. As a chef serving at the hatch, I was engaged the most, I guess because people had to talk to me about what they wanted, and then some realised it was me and often laughed to cover their embarrassment.

When I was debriefing with the teams afterwards, I reflected on these observations, and was sad to learn that most just accepted that this was a part of service life. But does it have to be like that? Shouldn't we respect everyone in the workplace and remember that they are all humans with families, feelings and interesting lives? Working in HR, these are the very people we should get to know, because they know exactly what the issues are, department by department, what is happening around the building, what the gossip is, who works hard and who is work-shy! If you look after them, they will look after you. And just a note in case you wondered: many of these groups were outsourced, but they were still part of the team, and therefore worth getting to know.

How awful is it that so many ignore the human beings working around them? How much is it to ask that more people, maybe you after reading this chapter, can take a few seconds to engage in eye contact, say a proper 'hello' and, when time permits, ask how they are doing and LISTEN to the reply?

18

Coaching

I find it remarkable that after many years of coaching being provided to managers and members of teams, that people still associate it with failure. I think that is, in part, due to the fact that years ago people were given coaching when they were failing in some aspect of their job. It was seen as a last chance to develop, change and make the grade, or be let go from the role they were in.

In today's business world there is obviously some coaching that continues to be provided to people who are in difficulty and need support, but far more are turning to coaching because they are known to be successful in what they do, and they want to reach even higher levels of success in their role.

The best coaches are usually accredited by a body that ensures they meet minimal standards and adhere to key practices, such as maintaining high levels of productivity. Most coaches are non-directive in their approach, helping the person see their own weaknesses and discover the best way to move forward with coaching. Sometimes it can also be about a strength, and how to exploit it better.

Coaches come in many varieties. Above I have described what tend to be termed executive coaches, who usually charge for a programme or course of meetings over a set timeframe, and have specific goals to be reached by the end. But there are also specialists who concentrate on areas such as presenting to large gatherings, handling press interviews, dealing with disciplinary and grievance situations, etc.

Some line managers question the cost of a coach, but my findings have always been that the cost of the coach is more than made up for by the gain in productivity of the coachee, and their acknowledgement of the investment in their development made in them, by their organisation.

19

Coffee

If you've just arrived at an organisation that doesn't have access to great coffee, then put that near the top of your priority list. Providing kettles and instant coffee just doesn't have the same impact as a dedicated coffee station, a proper machine that grinds beans to order and makes the cup whilst you wait. And it's the waiting that is key. This provides an opportunity for people hailing from different departments to gather around and chat, and it is that chatter that will lead to a better work environment, and sometimes improved communications and higher productivity. Some people will get into work earlier and stay later if you fulfil their needs and stop them having to go to a coffee shop on the way in or out. The caffeine in the coffee itself will help with productivity. Whatever you do, don't restrict the number of cups people can have. The cost is in the machine and its maintenance, the cost of the coffee itself is incidental, and the milk you were having to provide anyway.

In the UK, 'let's have a coffee' often turns into a cup of tea, but the opportunity is the same. It is the chance for two or more people to have a chat in a less formal atmosphere than a meeting in an office. It is the ideal way for a team leader to get to know their team better, as you have the chance to discuss issues outside of work, as well as projects hitting barriers within the organisation. When people talk about having too many meetings, they rarely mean coffee, and especially when it comes with cake.

When I worked at Wellcome Trust I wanted to make use of an area that was only at that time being used for the lunch service. We were lucky to have an exceptional account manager who sourced a coffee cart made of recycled yoghurt pots, made an arrangement for the supply of a specialist coffee, and found the most personable and engaging barista, Valentina Rinaldi (who is now the illustrator of my children's books). Very quickly people discovered the new space and started having chats with colleagues, and even held team meetings around the cart.

One of the Wellcome graduates introduced Randomised Coffee Trials, whereby those who wanted to put their name on a list were paired, by lucky dip, with another person and encouraged to have a coffee and chat about their jobs and interests. It proved to be a great way of cross-fertilising the whole organisation, and was later supported by other senior execs getting involved.

20

Communications

Almost every issue that has gone wrong in my working life can be pinned down to poor communications. Either the wrong people finding out in the wrong order, incomplete leaks of information, deliberate miscommunication or a lack of clarity in what was being communicated. When these things happen, the rumour mill takes over, and you're on the back foot. Which leads to the obvious conclusion that you need to plan your communications well, thinking about the audience and the timetable in advance. And if you possibly can afford to do so, consult with an internal communications expert first (either in-house, or a consultant).

Even with the risks, I have always tried to take people into my confidence about an issue or a change that is being considered. And 99% of the time it has paid off, with people both respecting the decision to bring them into the privileged position of being able to discuss and form the new structure or policy. The 1% is not always easy to predict. It can be the person that you trust the most that lets something slip, or feels the need to boast to someone about their insights into what is happening. But I have always argued that the 1% should not put us off the desire to be as inclusive as possible. After all, we are not planning a military attack, and lives are not normally on the line, albeit it can sometimes feel like that when redundancies have to be planned.

One of the most important teams to think about is your own. I have often brought the HR team into a planned communication early. Not only do they need to know, but they need to be ready to answer questions as soon as it goes live. Before that, they can quiz you on the nature and style of the communication and help you refine it, or help you predict the questions that are likely to be asked. Staff reps and unions can also help in this respect, provided that you have built up the necessary level of trust and understanding. On occasion I have managed to prepare the textbook comms exercise, such as when I shared the platform with colleagues from senior management and the trade unions to talk through and answer questions about a major restructuring. But that was a rare feat.

Having talked about the HR team, staff reps and senior managers, the other group that are often overlooked are the middle managers and the supervisors: the very people the majority of your workforce report in to. In many cases they are left out of the planning process and only hear when the rest of the staff hear. This inevitably leads to problems, as they then struggle to answer legitimate questions from their team while simultaneously trying to process the implications for themselves. I have seen this in the aftermath of a big merger, which had been kept secret from all but a handful of senior leaders for fear of the stock market hearing ahead of schedule.

The process thereafter can be messy, especially if you are having to use FAQs and Q&A sheets prepared by corporate lawyers with zero knowledge of your workforce. To get round this issue, plan phased announcements: all managers, then staff reps (even if they have already been engaged, they still need sight of the final announcement and any variances), then staff. Be ready for people to walk into HR to ask questions, to seek more detail. At the very least, collate all the questions and answer them on an open forum as soon as you can. That way you can keep on top of the rumour mill.

21

Conferences

There are a good range of HR conferences to choose from, and a variety of dates, lengths and times of the year. In the UK, the CIPD conference is held in conjunction with a large exhibition, where you can find out about the latest ideas and software, meet suppliers and, most importantly, find other professionals struggling with similar issues to you back at their workplace.

The conferences usually feature some well-known published authors giving speeches about their research, as well as some more practical seminars where other Human Resources professionals will share the details of projects they have undertaken.

If you get the chance to go, then take it, especially if your employer is willing to cover your costs. Even better, is to be invited to speak at a conference or seminar. This has happened to me several times, and it means that you don't have to pay the fees, and often your hotel and travel is also covered. An invite often follows the publication of a story about your company in a newspaper or journal, or an industry award, as the conference organisers rely on these for ideas for topics.

Increasingly, speakers now buy their place at a conference, often supported by their publisher, as it is a great way to promote their book, or for a consultant to promote their services. Sadly, this now applies to awards as well. Judges are no longer invited to review award submissions, but are asked to buy a seat on the panel alongside the promise that they will get a plug at the ceremony and publicity for themselves or their company. This might help explain some of the surprising choices for award winners, given how rigged the judging system has become! Having said that, awards are still a great way to honour a team that has worked on a project and had a successful outcome. Just the mere pleasure of taking a team to a dinner after being nominated is great fun, let alone the chance of being commended or winning.

At a conference I always take lots of notes as a way of getting the ideas into my head. There are often choices between seminars and some only allow you into the ones that you have pre-booked. If you discover you've made a mistake, don't feel strange about just getting up and leaving. No one knows what you're doing, or cares. There's no need to lose an hour of your life with a poor speaker or panel. Maybe move to another room, get a drink or catch up on email. You could also visit the exhibition, which will be quieter when the seminars are running.

The biggest reason for me to go, especially for those conferences over a few days, is to get to know other delegates, or other speakers. Some of these encounters have led to the opportunity to visit them at their place of work and learn more about the way they have tackled an issue. It's also meant I have been able to extend my network, which always comes in handy when you are looking for your next project, or know someone who is thinking about applying to that company. And it's probably why Zoom-type webinar conferences will be used for COVID times, but will be dropped when normality returns. Most people find it easier to meet others face-to-face, rather than electronically (or is that just a generational thing?). One tip though: be wary of conferences offered free on a cruise liner. You will pay many times over with your time as you get moved from one supplier to another. It's a high price for the dubious pleasure of listening to a small number of speakers at the actual conference part of the event.

22

Consulting Rates

Setting out as a consultant is a big move, but hopefully one you will enjoy, albeit you will need to give it at least six months to get going. The reason for this is that, unlike interim or permanent work, you will pick up a series of projects. Some will be intense for a short period, but many will be projects that spread over several months, part-time, supporting the businesses with your expertise, meaning you can handle several clients at once. To get to this stage will take a while. You will spend time making contacts, talking about what you can offer, making formal pitches and rarely getting approval for a project. To build up a portfolio of clients who trust you and want to work with you regularly takes more time than you can imagine. And if the economy takes a dive, you will be even more expendable than the other interim contractors or temporary staff on payroll.

Rates are tricky, to put it mildly, but you should be able to sell 100 billable days a year (the rest are spent marketing, phoning, drinking coffee, eating lunches, occasionally preparing and then giving pitches, training, holidays, researching and report writing). This is different to an interim, who will get a lower rate but many more days at a time (e.g. a three or six-month gig).

As a starting point, take your old gross salary and benefits and divide by 100, e.g. £30k plus pension is £33k, divide by 100 = £330 per day.

That's a first marker. Now find out what the market is paying. Chat to agencies. They will be happy to help, because they will want to sign you up for interim and project work under their umbrella. They may well be able to show that you could earn more (maybe your old salary didn't reflect your skills and experience?). You'll get less if you work at public organisations or at charities, but you will get references and some great contacts instead.

The real test comes when you pitch. You may have to negotiate, so start high. Don't forget that what you agree will stick for a while. Be ready to discount, e.g. every eleventh day free, but keep your rate, when it is set, as fixed as possible. If you get lots of work, push your rates up. And if you don't like a job, quote twice your normal rate. You might still get it!

23

Consulting Work

In some sectors of the economy it is quite legitimate to work as a consultant whilst holding down a regular job. This is particularly the case in the university sector, where tenured employees will have provisions built into their contracts that define the external work they can undertake, and on what terms that must be done. Not only does this add to their public sector income, but it also leads to opportunities for their university to collaborate.

Alternatively, some employers include clauses in their contracts that forbid their employees to work for anyone else. These clauses are written to protect their IP and business interests. Even if such a clause exists, it is still worth asking (provided that you cannot see a conflict of interest), since an enlightened boss may well see it as beneficial to your development. You might be asked to take holiday or unpaid leave, which begs the question about how much you should receive. Your day pay rate is probably annual salary divided by 240 (the number of working days in a year for a full-timer). If you can earn more than this on an external assignment, then well played. If you are supporting a charity and don't want to be paid anything but travel expenses, then your line manager might consent to the consulting being resolved as additional paid, or special, leave.

It's a small world, so always tell your employer. You never know who knows whom, and it may well get back to your boss anyway. Keep clear records of everything you do and remember to declare additional earnings to HMRC when you do your tax return (in the UK there is an 'other income' section).

24

Controlling Boss

A controlling boss to one person is often revered for the support they give by another. It may be that your boss doesn't realise you perceive them in this way. The key is to try to understand the motives for their behaviour. It's probably the case that they are trying too hard to ensure everything is just how they want it and that they, in turn, will look good to their boss.

The reasons for exercising control are many and various. Maybe they have had a bad experience in the past, or they don't want you to fail, or they are concerned about the customers who demand perfection. Of course, it might be a power play to keep you in your place!

Building trust is one way to ensure that things improve. Try going to them with 'I've just completed this report, is it okay for me to send it out?' or 'I'd like to send these out as soon as they are ready. What are your criteria for success?'. Similarly, with projects, list what you're doing and the rough time allocation for each and then ask if that is appropriate. Once you get the green light, their need for control will diminish. So, give things time to settle, try to discuss your concerns, and negotiate a way forward at your next private face-to-face meeting.

25

Crisis Planning

If you have just taken up the role as Head of HR, crisis planning is one of those things that does need to be dealt with relatively early on. Don't wait until someone from a central risk function asks you to update your old plans, if any exist. You never know when an issue will arise that leads to major changes needing to be made. Pre-COVID, people would talk about a fire in the workplace, a loss of data from a computer, or a bomb threat, but nowadays it will also include details about how to cope with furloughing staff and large numbers working at home.

As an HR team, we are often turned to in a crisis, especially when there is a need to contact people quickly, or talk to distressed relatives. We need to make sure our basic data is kept up to date. Where do people live? What are their home phone numbers (when the mobile doesn't work)? Who is their next of kin, or trusted person? People hate to be hassled and asked to update their HR records, but it has to be done, so make it a bit more fun, with every twentieth person to do so winning a small prize, or in extreme cases, withholding their pay until they confirm their bank details and the other numbers are correct!

I've been called upon several times in my career to help in a crisis. Researchers working in an African country where there was a military coup needed to be urgently contacted and given instructions on where to go for their evacuation. Meanwhile, their loved ones back home needed to be briefed on what was happening, and what we were doing to keep them safe. Another time volcanic dust stranded people around the globe, and the travel company realised they were overly reliant on emails, so we made the contacts, sometimes through personal mobiles. When the bombs went off in Central London, the mobile networks were either taken down by the security forces, or they failed due to overuse; we needed to use old-fashioned landlines to get messages around and help reassure both employees and their families. When we had a fire in a building with no entry control system, we didn't know who was in there at the time, so we phoned everyone and their emergency numbers, until we could confirm that the building was empty. And at its simplest, we used mobile texts to alert people to use the rear staff entrance, when protestors clogged up the street at the front entrance.

The following list is not exhaustive, but worth considering:

- Work with IT to remind people how to log-in and carry on working if travel is restricted; ensure Zoom or similar is installed and understood, maybe by using an occasional dummy run; make sure all data is regularly backed-up off site (these days often in the cloud).
- Work with finance to refresh rules for reimbursing mobile phone, broadband and home-working expenses when an issue demands it.
- Revise sickness rules to be flexible, and absence rules to cover people being stuck abroad, unable to travel.
- Work with facilities to ensure there are rehearsed plans in place for a building evacuation, and that people with mobility, or other, needs are looked after.
- Set up a phone line for people to call, or a private webpage for them, or their partners, to access latest news, just in case.
- Regularly update personal records for all staff, explaining why it is necessary.
- Consider evacuation insurance if you have people working in volatile environments who might need extraction.

- As the HR lead you will need to ensure there is an agreement about who will take control in the event of an illness or accident to any of your leadership team (like Rabb taking over from Johnson during COVID-19). Whilst I am no advocate of formal and complex succession plans, a clear chain of command is needed at the top of your organisation.
- Create a cascade system of call out, or use multiple text systems, to spread key messages quickly.
- Have an agreement within your own team about who is on duty at weekends, or during holiday periods, and make sure they have access to all the systems, and/or the offices if needs be.

26

Culture

Companies spend many thousands every year undertaking employee surveys and trying to understand, and then change, their culture. Surveys have their own limitations, but how do you really understand the culture of a place? In a small organisation of just a few people it might well be possible to describe the culture, but as soon as you pass a hundred or so employees, then you will find many different cultures. Finance have their own subculture embedded within the wider organisation, as do HR and all the other functions. There are also different cultures within departments. The service engineers, for example, live in a totally different world to their own admin support team.

When I have been asked if I could help change a culture, or join a culture-change programme, I have therefore always started with the question, 'What is it that you want to change, and what are your motives?' If you are not careful, you can pay the big consulting firms a lot of money to come in and measure the culture and then prescribe lots of fundamental changes that they believe are needed (and will bump the price up further to support making those changes), but they will always be related to their models and their methods, and may well not work in your organisation.

By asking what the desired change is, even if it is in multiple sections, you can then go out to the organisation and consult with groups in different departments and at different organisational levels, to understand their perception, what they believe is getting in the way of a better culture, and start to look at ways to fix the problems that are thrown up.

Often concerns about productivity underlie a desire by senior managers to change the culture. They are being asked by their exec team to produce more with less and need to find savings, or they are concerned about levels of turnover amongst groups of employees, or they have concerns about the working style of some of their supervisors (e.g. persistent claims of bullying). The key is to get to the bottom of what is happening and find the root cause of the issue.

Something like an increase in employee turnover can have its roots in a whole variety of reasons. In one case I dealt with it was a knock-on effect: after ten years being together as a team, one supervisor found a better job elsewhere and suddenly everyone got itchy feet and wanted to move on as well. In other cases, turnover is the result of poor line management, or in a bigger department it might be related to a lack of opportunity to progress or take part in interesting work. Each challenge has its own appropriate response or responses.

Using a 'WHY?' diagram can be quite helpful, either on a flip-chart with a group, or on a note-pad privately. It is simple but effective. Right in the centre of the paper, write a concise problem question, such as 'Coffee tastes bad'. Then ask the attendees to shout out in turn the main reasons and link them to the central bubble. You might have 'cheap coffee', 'plastic cups', 'sour milk' and 'dirty machine'. From these, push out further, always asking the WHY? question. 'Why is the coffee cheap?' Add a bubble: 'Budget cuts'. 'Why do we use plastic cups?' ... 'Because the dishwasher is broken.' Keep pushing further out: 'Why is the dishwasher broken?' ... 'Because the maintenance contract ended' ... 'Because of budget cuts.'

When you look at all the outer bubbles a picture starts to emerge, hopefully not about the coffee, but it might well reveal the budget cuts have led to the bad atmosphere in the group. Sometimes group meetings don't work and you need brave individuals to tell you, in confidence, about the real reason there is an issue, e.g. 'The new supervisor is arrogant, rude and only ever criticises our work.'

Once you have an understanding of the required change, then you need to think through possible solutions, involving a good number of the stakeholders as early as you can. Change is best achieved with everyone thinking it is their idea, or at least that they had a part in deciding what is needed and how it should be implemented. None of this is easy, and there are often unintended consequences of making changes, but the way that usually wins is by breaking a big issue down into smaller parts and picking them off, one by one, ensuring the changes are embedded before moving on to the next fix. And where there is genuine resistance to change, think about introducing a change in a time-limited trial: it's less threatening and therefore more acceptable to the majority to try something out, rather than have a permanent change forced upon them. If it doesn't work out in the way you expected, then you won't be losing face by abandoning the trial rather than a new policy or process.

At the whole organisation level the one thing I have experienced, again and again, is the impact made by a new CEO. I have seen one place move from being in the doldrums and accepting failure, to turn around and work its socks off for the new, enthusiastic and personable leader. Sadly, I have also seen a new CEO all but destroy a place, twice. In trying to explain these changes in culture, I often reference a failing sports team getting a new head coach or manager. Measuring results is much easier with sports teams, and when you hear from the dressing room the reasons about the turnaround it's nearly always that the new coach has generated a dynamic atmosphere and spoken to each player individually, reminding them about their strengths and giving them the confidence to go and express themselves. It's the same team, just better results, as the consequence of a change in culture takes effect.

CVs

During my time in HR I have seen way too many CVs that have lacked soul. They have followed a set format, dictated by a Word template, and have therefore blended into the scenery. A CV is your marketing leaflet: it only works if it gets you through the door to the interview. It should showcase your education and work experience, but also say something about you as a person. For that reason you should always include an insight into who you are outside the workplace in an Interests section. It might just make you stand out from the other people that share your qualifications and work history when the shortlisting is underway.

Try to keep your CV to a couple of pages, three at most. Avoid photos and other graphics, and once you have a layout that you like, save it as a PDF before sending it out, so that readers on different systems won't get a mashed-up format on their screen. If you are applying for both interim and permanent roles, think about creating two CVs that play to both audiences. The same is true for different sectors (the detail you might include in a life science CV is totally different to a media agency, for example). And always get at least two other people to check your spelling and grammar; don't rely on software.

Dignity

Dignity is an important value for HR professionals to uphold. The key to dignity is ensuring, as best as you are able, that people are treated fairly and reasonably within the workplace. The easiest way of measuring that is to ask yourself, if that was you, would you be happy that your treatment was fair and reasonable?

The cost of not maintaining dignity in the workplace is often seen in failing to retain the best people. If someone sees others being treated badly, then they will start thinking about moving to a better environment, quite rightly fearing they might be next on the list. This is especially true where bullying is taking place.

Unfortunately, dignity is often overlooked in the name of security. For example, a redundancy is about to be made in IT, and the line manager is concerned about a revenge attack on the systems on departure. The person is invited into the office and told they are redundant, and that they will be escorted out of the office, and that all their passes and passwords have all been expired. Consultation is out of the window and all dignity is removed. Not ideal!

Our job as HR professionals is to find a way to make this more palatable. It's not just about a generous settlement agreement. If we have tried to push back and the managers are insisting on this approach, then offering to meet the employee that evening and give them access to their desks to clear their personal belongings, or offering to meet them at a local café and talk through the redundancy, or helping with their CV, reference, networking, etc, can all help restore some dignity and reduce the pain (and maybe reduce the reputational damage that can follow). Team members will also want the chance to say goodbye, give a leaving present and sign a card. There is nothing wrong in helping make arrangements for a leaving do at a club or pub one evening after work to allow for a proper departure.

29

Diversity and Inclusion

There are whole books on this one topic. It's important to read some of them to understand all the intricacies. It's even more important to talk to other practitioners about what they have done, and how they achieved it. This is not an area where you should try to reinvent the wheel; it's better to learn from others, and avoid making some of their mistakes along the way. Once you have completed your review, you can start to propose changes. You may have more control over some aspects than others, such as ensuring greater fairness in your selection process, but these other aspects will require support from the wider organisation.

Think carefully about what you are trying to achieve and why. Even though some senior managers will play along, they will do so less than wholeheartedly, unless you can help them see that being inclusive is more for the longer term success of the organisation, bringing greater diversity in the way problems are tackled and showing to the world a healthy reflection of the wider population. Help them see how the business benefits and they will help you make the changes stick in the longer term.

Everywhere I have worked I have found people passionate about aspects of diversity and inclusion, especially where they have been personally impacted. And they are sprinkled throughout the organisation. The bigger the organisation, the more likely there will be people prepared to step forward and discuss attitudes to subjects such as race equality, trans or homophobia in the workplace, access for someone with hearing loss, or opportunities for women to progress. At Wellcome I had the opportunity to work with Lauren Couch, who completely turned my thinking on its head with her passion and deep, thoughtful insights into D&I. Your task is to find people like Lauren in your organisation and make them champions of change in this important field.

A great way to gain initial traction is to call for people to come forward and chat in an open forum about their experiences and insights, and to suggest opportunities to change for the better. Setting up some teams to reflect the interests of the people that step forward works well, with your task being to facilitate their meetings and represent their ideas to senior management where appropriate.

Many organisations put way too much effort into monitoring diversity, sending around lengthy surveys where people have to identify with a wide range of questions about their sexual orientation, their religious affiliation, their race, age and gender. They make comparisons with census data and other organisations' published data, or they join an organisation such as Stonewall to be able to make some comparisons, but my experience tells me that all this data does is tell you what you already knew. It's your actions that will make a difference. So, if one of your task-force members has had a good idea about an aspect of diversity or inclusion, and you can see a way of making it happen, then do so and more people will then be encouraged to engage, and change will surely follow.

An announcement that the exec team have agreed that all interview panels will feature at least one member of each sex, as will shortlists of candidates, and that directors will want to understand why there is no ethnic diversity in a recruitment programme for half a dozen trainees, will always lend more weight, and create more discussion and interest, than someone trying to explain on the internet why there is a gender pay gap.

How do you win over the exec team in the first place? This is a tough one. Part of the issue is that many execs read the paper put to them, express interest and ask questions at the meeting, and then do the bare minimum, claiming that if they don't attend to their primary function, then there won't be a business left to try to create an inclusive environment in. Some, of course, are bigots, but mostly they are just lazy and need constant encouragement and engagement.

The key is the quality of the business case that you put forward. What is it that the organisation will lose out on by failing to tackle diversity and inclusion? Is it customers, or in a research organisation might it be a loss of ideas or appropriate challenges? Your task is to help the execs see what they will miss out on, e.g. in a university it might be that a less inclusive department attracts poorer staff and ultimately fewer, or less able, students as the quality of research drops.

Sometimes the only way is to build change from within the management and 'shame' the execs into action. Other times the NEDs (non-executive directors) need to play a part, perhaps by making bonuses dependent upon hitting diversity targets, such as the gender pay gap, as exemplified by the Trustee Savings Bank. And there are times, of course, where the organisation can rise up and make the views of the execs all but irrelevant, something that has started to happen in corporate America.

30

Dogs

One of the simplest and yet most rewarding and memorable work days for me, was not linked to the introduction of a new pay scheme, or the launch of a new policy, it was a day when a range of working dogs were invited into the building at lunchtime to meet staff. When I would run a lunchtime meeting about a subject like wellbeing, I'd get a reasonable number of people coming along, but dogs bring everyone out, it seems!

We had a guide dog in training, a companion dog at a care home, a dog that sniffed out narcotics (which some people didn't want to go near!) and another that could detect gas leaks. Finally, we had a dog that could detect some forms of cancer, and again it was interesting that there were only a few people that wanted to interact with it, maybe fearing the worst.

Some offices are now experimenting with giving people the opportunity to take their dogs into work with them. The dog benefits by not being left at home, and enjoying the attention that it receives from the owner and other staff, but I do wonder if it stresses some breeds out, and I'm equally not sure that it's ideal for a dog to commute long distances by car or public transport. Where you have to say no, however, is if you get a barker or a runner. They are way too distracting and will lead to a reduction in productivity, or worse if you have an employee with an allergy.

31

Emails

Many people struggle with 24/7 mobile devices and the feeling that they have to respond to, or at least keep on top of, the ever-growing mountain of communication. There is no simple answer to a full inbox, but here are some thoughts:

- Set up a filter (YouTube it) that separates email that you are only copied into. You can skim that later, whilst paying immediate attention to the mail addressed to you.
- Consider an auto-reply such as 'I've received much more email than normal recently, please allow me some extra time to respond', but do change this regularly, as it becomes meaningless after a few days, especially if used with an internal audience.
- Don't respond immediately to enquiries, especially where there are others included in the 'To' address, otherwise you'll get caught by follow-up questions (many issues resolve themselves given a bit of time and the input of others).
- Take a three-week holiday and tell everyone you're not going to look at emails or work things during that time. Only by having a lengthy break do people start to realise that they can make their own decisions.
- Tell everyone you won't review work email at weekends and then stick to it, and for holidays that you'll accept texts only in an emergency.

- In terms of best practice, try to set a good example. Only CC people in who really have to see the message, otherwise save their inbox from getting too full. This applies particularly to Reply All: could you just reply to the sender instead? Don't send or answer emails in the late evening (or weekends), unless there is a genuine time-sensitive issue that *has* to be dealt with. If you're in a senior position, then people will feel they have to respond and so the vicious cycle ramps up.

32

Engagement

For those who don't work in either Human Resources or Internal Communications, 'engagement' in this chapter isn't the act of declaring love or commitment prior to marriage that is practised in some societies, nor is it a diary commitment. Instead it is a reference to the efforts made to get interaction going between the organisation and its employees.

Many HR teams believe the only way to measure and manage engagement in a workforce is to run an annual staff survey. It goes something like this:

The sales rep turns up and displays a range of glorious charts that show the mean-average scores for a wide range of attitudes in lots of similar companies, and explains that you will get deep rich data into your organisation and instantly understand what needs to be prioritised. Contracts are agreed and initial communications go out to let people know a survey will occur between two set dates. The date arrives and each employee gets their email, often with a direct link to the provider's database. Some people complete it as soon as it arrives, others hold back, wondering if their own scores and comments will get back to their line manager (regardless of the comms, which state that everything is anonymous). Others ignore it completely.

The deadline arrives, and the internal teams driving the project go into full panic mode trying to cajole those who haven't submitted their survey to take action. Unfortunately, they wind up all the people who completed early on by sending out all-staff messages, or they target only those that haven't replied and confirm suspicions that the survey is being monitored!

The data is then processed by the survey company. Several weeks later, after checking all is in order, they send a draft report of the basic scores, but not the detail, and very little commentary. You're told that your engagement score is seventy, say. Which is meaningless until you compare with similar companies, or pay them for a presenter to come and explain what it means.

When the next set of data arrives after another week, you learn more about the make-up of the numbers and what the major issues are (or the 'key drivers' as they call them). You share it with your directors, and they suggest that more analysis is needed before it is released to staff. They also ask for data for their division, again possibly at extra cost.

High up on the list is always communications. No company that is bigger than twenty in size needs to be told this, but the survey companies thrive on it. They have action lists and opportunities for further surveys to help improve your comms. Oh yes, they do!

Having looked at the data, you're now trying to work out which division has the biggest issue. 'No problem,' says the survey company, 'for an extra charge we can break it down to any subset that is at least ten people or more in size.' Another fortnight passes.

Finally, you have the courage to send out an all-employee announcement that the data is back and will be presented in a couple of weeks at a town hall meeting. Given that three months have now passed, most people have forgotten about the survey, but some dutifully show up, and are immediately disappointed to be told about obvious problems, and that there is no action plan to solve them, other than 'We are forming some task groups and working project teams to review the data and propose a course of action'.

The reality is that the data is usually all over the place, it leaves more questions than it answers, and it winds up the very employees that you are trying to 'engage' with. Why? Put simply, running a survey of attitudes suggests that the company accepts that change is needed, and that something will be done as a consequence, which is exactly what they don't see happening!

What are the alternatives to surveys, or how do you at least increase the engagement scores in your surveys? The easiest answer is to think of engagement as proper adult two-way communication between line managers and their teams. At the top, this means regular presentations by the CEO to the whole organisation with proper Q&A sessions (try giving people the opportunity to submit anonymous written questions to open up the dialogue, if you only get a few people contributing). This should flow down through the organisation, with directors addressing their divisions, and managers their teams.

To achieve this considerable help is needed, especially in training and developing those being asked to talk with their teams. It helps if the people at the top lead by example and take the feedback seriously, rather than spend all their time being defensive and creating excuses. Post-event rationalisation is a phrase that comes to mind. Here's a great example I heard: 'Well, we should have known that the announcement of the new CFO would upset people, and that's why the scores are so low in that division.'

HR folk can also play their own part. Instead of just working in their office and only talking to people who make appointments, they can spend a day each week working at desks with their client teams, going to coffee and lunch with them, and generally getting to know them until the trust develops to discuss the meatier issues. Then a few weeks later, by stopping by and asking after a sick child or exam results, all ways of showing that they listen and care.

HR can also be instrumental in forming topic-specific focus groups, staff consultative groups, and/or regular open meetings with the trade unions. Again, by listening to and taking action on the smaller things (like the type of toilet roll, or the quality of the coffee or sandwiches), people will be more open to talk about bigger things like reward or working hours.

I've also tried, with some success during a merger, installing an anonymous graffiti wall, albeit the security camera nearby had to have a bag put over it to convince people they weren't being watched! The seeding question was, 'If you were sitting on the plane next to our new CEO, what would you say to him?' The first few days were silly, with responses ranging from 'Gee, is this what First Class is like?' to 'Can I eat your nuts?' to 'I like your socks.' But we kept our promise and published every response on the intranet (except those defaming individuals, which thankfully were few in number).

Within a week we were getting some high-quality proposals for change and challenges to the way things were run, and people were putting their names to their comments. And the trick here was to get the divisional director to give responses, even if some were supported by suggestions from comms and HR. Change happened and trust and confidence grew, and eventually people were regularly leaving great ideas and their names.

Enthusiasm

A loss of enthusiasm from a member of your team, or another member of staff that you're providing support to, can arise from a wide range of possible issues. More often than not it's a cyclic thing that will resolve itself, but this can never be taken for granted, especially amongst those people that need new stimuli on a regular basis.

The first thing to check is that it is real, and not just your perception. State what your perception is in a private meeting, and listen to the response. I've been amazed at how often an employee doesn't realise they have been underperforming, and have misinterpreted or misunderstood feedback that they've had as just an interest in their current project by their manager. There may be some underlying reasons in their private life or in their health, so be ready to listen and to accommodate as needed.

If appropriate, set some realistic and achievable targets and explain that you want to review them regularly, and then set some dates for follow-up meetings in their diary.

Maybe help them find a mentor, or provide a coach for a short period. By helping, others will recognise your compassion.

Alternatives include helping in a new project, attending a new training programme, undertaking a secondment to another team, taking a sabbatical break, or even providing CV help and references to move on.

Exiting

It's a classic situation that many find themselves in, torn between a loyalty to the organisation, to their boss, or to their staff or customers, versus their own need to progress and/or get fulfilment from their work.

The first thing to remember, especially in larger businesses, is that you will be dropped in a heartbeat if the organisation needs to reduce its costs, or it merges, or it changes direction, or it feels you aren't pulling your weight.

You really do have to be a bit selfish, think through all the things you want from a change, seek the help of close friends or a mentor, and then start applying for new roles externally, or setting out on your own.

Having said all of that it is, however, sometimes best to start where you work. And that's because you have already proved yourself to the organisation and people know you. Set out what you would now love to do with your line manager, show your passion and interest, and maybe start by taking on a short-term project to see if it works for you and others. It might be that you can find a new, reinvigorating role at your current workplace and therefore keep all your benefits and continuity of service.

The key thing to remember is that if you do leave, or move on internally, others will have the chance to up their game and fill the space you have left, and people who needed your support can still come to you for a chat in the transition phase, or become your mentees. The wider organisation will have benefitted from your time with them, and will now benefit from a new structure taking over.

Feedback

There are times when you will need to get a team member to change their behaviour, for example, to stop being aggressive to other team members. To achieve this, you will need to avoid being confrontational, and find a private and confidential way to get the message across.

Often the best way to deal with this is to arrange a face-to-face meeting in a neutral location. This doesn't have to be a booked room in the office building, or your office, especially if that would be out of the ordinary and raise suspicion. It could be in a local café, where you can often have a confidential chat simply because so many other people are there, or sometimes walking in a park.

Once you have put the team member at ease, take him through an example of an issue that you have witnessed yourself and that you can own (best to avoid third-party references if you can).

The key word to use is 'perception'. This avoids conflict: 'It is my perception that you are struggling to contain your temper, for example, I witnessed the way that you approached XYZ.'

Role play can be useful in these circumstances. Ask him to put himself in the shoes of the other person, to think about their issues, what is on their plate at the moment, and then you role play the way that he handled it so he feels the full force of his behaviour.

On more than one occasion I have had to help a person like this accept that they are much brighter and clever than the people they are having a hard time with, and that their task is to accommodate those people in the team by helping and encouraging them, rather than getting cross with them. This is particularly true when dealing with arrogance.

Having talked through some examples, and helped him understand the impact he is having on the team, chances are he will willingly accept the opportunity to receive some counselling, support or coaching. Re-affirm that you value him as a team member, and that you personally want to resolve this quickly, so that it doesn't become a bigger issue. Then find a coach, and be prepared to pay a reasonable price for a qualified and experienced person who can quickly turn them around. This is one of those occasions when you need an external person, rather than an in-house resource.

36

Finance

Something I learned early on in my HR career was that a good relationship with the finance team is beneficial to both the HR team and the organisation as a whole, and if it's toxic to look for an escape route, as I have had to do on a couple of occasions!

I've always explained to my finance partner that budgeting and keeping track of finances is not my forte, but I will work hard to agree and then keep to a budget, given the appropriate support. A great example for me was the opportunity to work with CFO Susan Lowther at RiboTargets. Not only did she run a tight ship, but she was always ready to explain in plain English and layman's terms, what was happening with the company's finances and share options. In return I have worked hard to keep finance confidentially up to date with proposed changes to the organisation, so that they can be prepared to provide support as needed to the CEO and top team.

In most organisations there is a constant expectation that running costs will keep decreasing, so asking for a level budget can be challenging, let alone asking for more. To do so you need to think from the perspective of the CEO. What will be the return on investment for the business of you providing an extra service? How will it be measured? Who will benefit? Sometimes you need to ask for a temporary increase to cover a new initiative, such as introducing a more powerful IT system. Other times it is to reduce the workload of your talented scientists, artists or innovators. An extra person in talent acquisition and retention might improve the people you're able to recruit and keep those that are productive for longer. What price can be put on that for the business?

Changes in legislation, the need for more accurate reporting, an increase in coaching support for senior leaders, all can lead to a requirement for more resources, but you must be able to show how and when you will bring costs down once the initiatives are embedded, and then follow through. And that is why it is sometimes best to hire someone in a temporary project role, rather than make an additional permanent appointment that will add to your fixed costs.

37

First HR Job

Whenever people ask me how to score that coveted first role in HR, I always start by saying that persistence is key. Many people chase every HR vacancy, but someone will get it, so keep trying.

If the person you're advising is just starting out, they should consider apprenticeships, volunteering for internships, and looking for temporary cover opportunities, especially in the bigger companies. Letting LinkedIn know that's what they want will also help, as will searching every day, as some vacancies come up and then close quickly, particularly in the private sector where there are no rules about advertising for a minimum number of days or weeks. Suggest they find friends of friends in HR and offer to buy them a coffee for a chat about how to get in. It's amazing how often the best jobs, work experience or training opportunities come from word of mouth.

Enrolling for a CIPD HR course, or similar, shows commitment, and will help them meet others working in HR departments and therefore hear first about opportunities.

If they are already in work, suggest they ask about secondments into HR in their current company, or volunteer to get involved in people projects, join the employee representative forum, chat to members of the HR team and let them know they're interested.

And then I would get them to read *Maverick!* by Ricardo Semler (it's old, but still the best book on people practices, and will give them some ideas to discuss when they get their first interview), or *The Prince* by Niccolo Machiavelli, to understand a bit more about humans and how they operate.

I always end by saying that the best thing they can do, if they are lucky enough to get to talk to an HR manager or Director, or even better, get an interview, is to stand out from the crowd by *avoiding* saying that they've 'always wanted to work with people'.

38

Gender Pay Gap

Governments around the world have finally woken up to the gaps in pay between men and women with similar experience in the workforce. In the UK, organisations have to publish the percentage difference between basic pay levels and bonuses, and then provide a narrative to explain the difference, describing the remedies they are putting in place to reduce the gap.

Human Resources is the team turned to by senior management to provide both the figures and, in most cases, the commentary. It is important that the task isn't completely delegated to HR to act and resolve on its own, because the people who can actively help reduce the gap are the executive team themselves. Even if you, as HR, are preparing the drafts, make sure they are signed off by the exec team.

The mistake some companies have made is to comply with the request to publish on the Government website, and then attempt to walk away. This approach is doomed to failure, unless the gap is tiny. Team members will find the data, in the same way that they find the annual report and shareholder communications, and they will want to ask questions and will often have suggestions about how the gap can be reduced.

The best approach, therefore, is to be upfront with employees about the results, as soon as they are known, and before they are officially published. If you have a consultative forum, or an agreement that includes regular discussions with trade unions, then use this as an opportunity to hold a discussion, and then follow it up by reviewing the suggestions made by them at the next executive meeting. If you don't have a staff forum, then this and staff wellbeing are effective ways to get one started.

If you want some inspiration about actions to take, search the internet for gender pay gap report actions, and you'll find plenty of great ideas.

39

Glassdoor

Used widely in the States, and starting to gain a significant foothold in the UK, Glassdoor is a social media site where you can read reviews of employers from both interview candidates and employees (current and ex). Take everything you read with a pinch of salt: bad reviews tend to be written by disgruntled ex-employees, and overly glowing ones can sometimes be traced back to PR or HR. Keep an eye open for your own organisation, and be ready to give a response to negative feedback, so that readers can set it in context.

40

Graffiti Walls

A simple idea. At time of change, or when a new programme or initiative is launched, put a large poster up on a wall in a communal area (it can be a roll of cheap brown paper), together with some felt tip pens, and a question or statement to start people going. That might be something like 'Tell us what you think of the new bonus scheme.' Make sure that the poster isn't under the eye of an obvious security camera, and then ask someone in another group to start to populate it, just to get it going. Allow anonymous responses, and don't remove them, unless they are deeply offensive or a personal attack on a colleague.

The temptation these days is to do everything like this online, but the beauty of a 'graffiti wall' is that people will put up comments without the threat of being challenged by managers later. Some will type and print and then paste their responses, for fear that their handwriting will be recognised, but provided you respect the responses and are seen to make appropriate changes to the scheme or programme you're inviting comments on, people will grow in confidence and eventually will put their name with their response.

Grey

To be successful in Human Resources you have to be able to play in the space between black and white. HR people who crave defined rules and regulations and spend their lives reviewing and redefining policies will lose the respect of the organisation, and eventually will struggle to develop. They will be labelled as pen-pushers, form-fillers or the rule-book police. Real life is rarely black and white.

The most obvious examples can be found in the absence section of any company handbook or set of rules and procedures. Whilst it is fine to say that employees will, or must, phone in on the first day of sickness, would you really discipline someone who has been taken to hospital and has no signal?

When writing or reviewing policies and procedures, pay special attention to the use of words like 'should' and 'will' or 'must'. There is a huge difference in your ability to take appropriate action if you have used a word like 'might' or 'should', instead of 'will' or 'must'. 'Should' gives you the chance to vary the rule as needed and try to be reasonable where there are mitigating circumstances, but it denies you the chance to be firm in a disciplinary sense, as it allows for wriggle-room (a technical term).

In all my years in HR, the steepest learning curve I have witnessed for new entrants to the profession is, without doubt, the ability to move away from trying to interpret the rules of the organisation and start to help people make their own judgements about the guidelines.

Holiday Cancellation

On rare occasions, like a merger or major restructuring, it may be sensible to reset your holiday dates and your employer should willingly cover your postponement costs. Note I said 'rare'! Sadly, I know of too many people who are no longer alive today because they didn't take the need for regular breaks seriously, or allowed their work to build up to such a level that they could never take their eye off their phone or laptop whilst away.

You have to remember there are bigger things in life than work. And you will find this out the day they no longer need you, or the day you are hospitalised!

If your work levels start to build up, you owe it to yourself and your family to start to prioritise, and do a great job of a smaller number of things, rather than try to tackle everything. Try saying 'I'm not going to be able to deal with this in the next few weeks because I have an exceptionally large workload and I have a family holiday booked in XYZ'. If they really need it doing *now*, then another route will open up. It's all about being honest: no one else knows what your workload is, you have to tell them.

And if you get no support, then take the hint and look elsewhere.

Home Working

In my experience, productivity increases when people are treated like adults, and are allowed to choose when to work from home, and when to join meetings in person. People are delighted to be spared the commute, and often the danger is that they work too hard when at home, trying to prove that they are doing a great job.

If you are just starting out on this path, then try a defined trial period and some guidelines for everyone to adhere to. You might start with a day a week and build up. If it doesn't work out after, say, three months, then you revert to your old practices, but chances are that everyone will work hard to make sure it works.

You do need to be able to resolve technical issues, like having sufficient laptops and how calls will be made (Zoom and Skype work fine), and if working at home becomes regular, then there may be a need for an assessment of their home workspace (e.g. for DSE regulations). The real key is that you trust your team and don't check up on them, and let them know that tea breaks, lunch, putting on the washing and accepting deliveries are all allowed.

COVID-19 probably means that this chapter seems like advice given in the last century, but I will leave it here for posterity. Indeed, the questions that are raised by home working (for those not furloughed) relate more to ensuring proper breaks, ways to ensure that young children and pets can be factored into the workload, and issues of confidentiality when people from more than one company are flat or house-sharing. There are no straightforward answers, and there is no way to write a rule book. The only way is to be flexible and ensure there is a budget for decent headsets, mice that can relieve RSI, sufficiently powerful machines, broadband connectivity, and an IT team specifically trained in offsite support techniques when things go wrong.

44

HR Strategy

There are many published books on the subject of HR strategy. So much so that some CEOs will expect you to have a strategy in place quite soon after you take on a leadership role, albeit they won't necessarily know a good one from a bad one, or one that is tailored for their organisation, versus one that has been lifted from the internet.

Even if you're not asked to provide one, it can be a good exercise to undertake with an HR team. You can involve the whole organisation, calling for those interested to join discussion groups and explore the culture of the organisation.

A great starting point is to get people to envisage what the company might look like if everything was perfect. Note down all the elements on a flip chart or similar, and vote on which are the most important. Once you have something to aim for, ask them to describe where they are now. Again, take notes and agree on the main issues. Once completed you have a ready-made gap. The vision of what perfect looks like and how to get there from the current situation can then be encompassed in your strategy document, alongside ways that you will measure progress and the timelines you will shoot for. Easy peasy! Once you have a first draft, it needs to be socialised with progressively more senior managers, and eventually endorsed and supported by the executive team. Without amendment and eventual buy-in from the senior leaders, it won't be worth a candle.

Having a strategy, a vision of what you are aiming for, can help lift the spirits of an HR team, who otherwise might grow despondent about fighting a seemingly endless battle of keeping on top of the basics and responding to events and changes made by the organisation and external environment. Equally, if handled badly, it can be a demotivator if people believe the strategy is the only way forward, and that no new projects will be entertained 'because they don't have sign-off from the executive team'. Keep it as a living, changing document, as you do objectives. That way it is there as a means of signposting the way forward and setting the principles and culture for the organisation to be guided by, as opposed to a set of rules that have to be followed at all costs.

Human Library

When trying to help your organisation become more inclusive, one of the best ways to help people understand the wide range of different issues that people face is to invite a Human Library into the offices. The idea is simple: people with interesting differences visit and take it in turns to chat to members of staff about their specific quality or skill. In library terms, they sit on the shelf until taken down by an inquisitive person. There then follows a conversation where questions are asked, and by the end of a fifteen-minute session, your team members have a better understanding of a disability or a state of being, which could include someone who has autism, Tourette's, is blind, transgender, ADHD – the possibilities are endless.

Interim Work

In the 19th and 20th centuries, jobs were often for life, and people made a career of steadily progressing through the ranks in one organisation. Today there's a healthy mix of permanent employees who have moved between companies, contract employees, temporary staff, apprentices, interns, interims and consultants. Interims can be attractive to companies as a means of employing an expert for a short period, without the employment law implications of a permanent role.

Interims tend to move from one role to another, spending four or five days a week engaged on a specific project as an expert with skills or knowledge that the current team doesn't possess, providing cover for someone on lengthy leave (maternity, paternity or sickness) or filling the gap between one person leaving and a new person arriving.

If you're thinking about becoming an interim then there several attractions: you can pick and choose where you work; you can take extended breaks between assignments for that four-week holiday on the other side of the world without any work emails; you can work full-on and get instant feedback from the people paying your bills; you'll be able to make a difference and then move on; you'll have a small number of focussed areas to work on and not carry any long-term baggage; you'll have clear objectives and a timeline to work to; you'll quickly build a strong network; you should be paid reasonably well; and you'll enjoy the variety that it brings.

Once you find something and get involved, you will need to build trust fast and get up to speed quickly, often living out of a suitcase in a hotel or Airbnb (but take care that you don't fall into the trap of working 24/7 just because you're away from home). You'll need to check that you have professional indemnity insurance or similar (CIPD has some useful links), and you'll need to be aware of tax issues (e.g. IR35 in the UK at the time of writing).

There are some potential downsides. Often you will leave one role and take that much needed holiday, only to return to find that there is nothing suitable for a few weeks or months. It can also be somewhat demoralising to put in a good spell at a place and then leave, to watch the new incumbent claim all the glory for the foundations you laid (but remember that is your role as an interim). Not everyone enjoys working with interims. They are either suspicious, or they treat you as a temp, not including you in any of the social activities of the group. Having said that, if you are acting as an interim that keeps getting extended, then there can be tax implications if you start to attend all the employee social events! Perhaps the biggest downside for me has been the development of excellent professional relationships with work colleagues that then have to be cut short, as you move on to the next role.

To succeed as an interim, you need to work hard on your networking, and keep it alive at all times, never knowing where the next lead will come from. There are a good number of agencies and search firms that specialise on interim placements. In the HR field, for example, both Caroline Clarke and Natalie Allen are always on top of their game, knowing who is going where, and what vacancies are on the horizon. Get to know them and work out which are the best consultants. Once found, keep in touch, even when you have work. If an agency finds you a suitable role, they will most likely invoice the client monthly and then pay you, having deducted their margin. Rarely they will receive a one-off placement fee for finding you and then leave you to the relationship, e.g. going onto the organisation's books or contracting via invoices.

Rates of pay as an interim vary considerably. If you are the hiring manager, remember that you will be saving on all your normal costs when you see the day rate being put forward by the agency or the consultant. Let them know how long you want the contract to run, what the deliverables are, your overall budget, and then see who is available and what prices are being quoted. Sometimes a more expensive, more experienced, interim can get the job done more efficiently and effectively than a cheaper alternative, so keep all these things in mind. Remember that most interims have chosen that way of life and are not a shoe-in to turn permanent later on, unless you make them an offer they can't refuse.

If you are the interim, then an effective way to evaluate your day rate is to take your old gross remuneration (including pension contribution and cost of healthcare, etc) and divide by 100. Use this as a rough starting point, and be ready to discount for lengthy contracts. Talk to interim agencies, let them see your CV, and find out what they think they could charge you out for. That will also help you work out what you can charge, remembering that the market is in constant flux, and rates are always going up and down dependent upon demand.

47

Interview Tactics

The real trick in an interview situation is to see if you can turn it into more of a conversation, so that you ask questions as you go along. This isn't always easy, especially when there is a panel interviewing you, but the main thing to remember is that an interview has to be a two-way process. You need to decide whether you want to work at the company that is interviewing you, as much as they have to decide if you fit their needs. So, what matters most to you, personally?

If it is your own development at this stage, then finding out how they will support you with training courses, getting involved in, or running projects, might be a key area to ask about.

If you have specific flexibility needs, then ask about their attitude to working from home, or taking time off and working extra hours at other times, or about their use of mobile technology.

Asking questions about pay and benefits should be low on your list. They can come later once you have them hooked, and they are making an offer. However, asking the interviewer to tell you what their perception of the culture is can be quite revealing. If they struggle with this, or offer platitudes, then ask some specifics: find out how decisions are made; which committees are important; is there any form of consultation; what are their current levels of turnover; what are they doing about their gender pay gap (that you looked up before coming to interview); and how do they feel about the comments about lack of diversity (or whatever has been raised) posted on Glassdoor?

And finally, if there is something you are uncomfortable about, then just ask. Isn't it better to rule yourself out now, rather than three months into the new job?

When answering questions, try to answer the question! This might sound obvious, but I've been amazed at how many times HR candidates have decided to behave like politicians, and answer my question with pre-prepared responses which are often gibberish when set against the question. Answer the question and, when giving examples, talk about the role that you personally played, rather than the role the team played. If you can hint at something interesting in your answer, this will lead to a follow-up question, and the interview will morph into a conversation.

48

Interview Nerves

It's actually more common than you think to suffer from nerves during an interview, and a good interviewer will know that you're excited about the job if you seem nervous. Never forget that in a panel situation, one or more of the panellists might also be nervous, not wanting to show themselves up in front of their colleagues.

The first thing is to be honest. Right at the start, explain that you get nervous in interviews. A good interviewer will support you. I once had a candidate who couldn't even speak. After taking him for a walk out of the office to get some water, he was able to relax and started to chat. If you can relax there's a much better chance of giving a great interview. And if they don't want to help you, do you really want to work there anyway?

It's perfectly acceptable to go into an interview with notes. So maybe take in a folder containing your CV and some bullet points to remind you of your relevant key experiences and projects. Open this up at the beginning and refer to it if the nerves kick in. If you are being interviewed by Skype or Zoom, then you can put your notes up as flipcharts behind the camera, so the interviewers will never know you are using them.

Take a sip of water, take some breaths, and just occasionally buy some thinking time by repeating the question before answering it (but not too often).

If everything goes wrong, consider sending a note afterwards saying you're sorry that your nerves took over and thank them for their support. If they didn't fill the vacancy, they might just call you back for a second chance, and then the likelihood is that your nerves will disappear.

IT Systems

I've worked with numerous IT systems in many different environments and none have been of any real use, so it is hard for me to recommend one.

My advice is to either follow the lead of the whole company ERP (Enterprise Resource Planning software) and bolt on a system that has been proven to work alongside it, or to find something that is compatible or integrated with the system your finance team uses. If you follow one of these routes, then the budget should always be available for the inevitable 'upgrade' (even cloud systems need customisation).

There is a whole industry being built around 'people analytics' and, scarily, some companies are making decisions based on the data they get out. The issue is that it is only as good as the quality of the data put in, how clean that data is, and how people have manipulated it to prove (or score) a point.

Even something as straightforward as sickness data is prone to abuse, misuse and all sorts of errors, leading to spurious claims or changes to systems and processes that weren't needed. And these errors are compounded when line managers have a people performance measure in their bonus plan, for example, employees being persuaded not to record stress or mental health issues and instead enter related reasons such as stomach ache or migraine.

Job Hunting

Just a few years ago papers, magazines and job boards held the majority of vacancies, but now recruiters are either finding talent directly through agencies or by conducting their own searches, using tools such as LinkedIn and web-crawling.

Before looking, make sure you have exhausted your current employer first. Are there any internal moves that you could make, projects you could volunteer for, extra responsibilities you could undertake to enrich your current experience and keep you going for a bit longer?

If you are going to move on, then get your CV right first, and know what it is that you're looking for. This is an appropriate time to have a confidential chat with one or more of your mentors, and your partner, especially if a move or change in work habits is contemplated.

Next up is your LinkedIn profile. Does it have enough information to ensure that a recruiter can easily evaluate your experiences, your qualifications and some data about your roles? Can you arm-twist a few people to give you a recommendation? Once all these things are in place, head to the profile section and click the box that says you are actively looking for vacancies, and answer the questions about role titles and locations that you'd consider. When suitable vacancies start to post in your feed (often overnight) then click and review them every day. In that way the algorithm starts to work for you, and directs even more opportunities your way. I have experienced this the wrong way round: I was looking on LinkedIn for opportunities for a mentee who wanted to be an HRBP and then received countless emails and leads for weeks afterwards, with nothing at the HRD level I personally required.

Searching for vacancies online takes time, but often uncovers fresh sources. Some bigger organisations have their own recruitment sites, as do the search agencies, and job vacancy sites will often pull data together from many places. Try many different search terms as you try to fish them out.

Let contacts and friends know you are ready for a move. Never ask them for jobs; just let them know what you are looking for, and many will forward relevant opportunities to you as they arise. Indeed, most of my opportunities have come from people I know alerting me to a vacancy, after I have told them I'm starting to look again.

Jobs in Smaller Companies

The biggest differences I've found about working in smaller organisations were the relative lack of rules and procedures, the need to roll up your sleeves and get on and do stuff (much of it nothing to do with HR), the critical importance of the management team, and the value of shareholders' money (especially when working for a company that wasn't yet generating any profits).

What made my move to RiboTargets from Glaxo so pleasurable was the quality of people in that team of forty-plus people. At Glaxo I was a deep expert in people stuff, whereas now I was treated as an equal member of an executive team with a broad input into all things management and leadership.

Before committing to a smaller company, you need to be confident the senior team hold similar values, so make sure you interview them as much as they interview you. The CEO plays a huge part in creating the culture. If you need to work to rules and dislike ambiguity, or your ideas always cost lots of money to implement, then steer clear!

When I later switched back to a bigger organisation, the extra confidence I'd gained in my knowledge of the wider business, especially finance (due to excellent tuition from RiboTargets CFO Susan Lowther), set me up well to play a full leadership role.

Key Performance Indicators

I have had a love-hate relationship with key performance indicators my entire working life. The worst is inheriting a set of KPIs that have been foisted on HR from another division, usually finance. They have to be produced on a regular basis and have to be reviewed every year, but try to reduce them in number and someone will always kick up a fuss. The only simple response is to try and amend them so that they can be fed by automated systems, or at worst by only small amounts of effort by the team. Whatever you do, don't allow them to go unchallenged, and push back if big policy changes are being demanded on the back of them. Remember they are only a snapshot of a specific measure made at a specific time, and they can never replace a decision based on a full review of all the pertinent facts.

Lateness

When someone is persistently late, don't jump to conclusions. The first thing you have to do is have a gentle private chat. Say you've noticed he has been in late quite often recently (don't formalise by stating dates and times at this stage) and ask if all is well. Then go quiet, don't fill the void (if there is one) by chatting, instead give him time to compose himself and tell you what he wants to.

I've been here many times in life, and the reasons can be annoying and fixable (the trains are messing up, my car share has ceased to be, my bike is being repaired); or sometimes they can be serious, such as my partner or parent is ill, my son is being bullied on the way to school so I need to take him, or I'm having to go to the doctors for a regular blood pressure test and they don't open till 8 am. Sometimes they can be annoying for another reason, for instance, he admits he's been going for interviews!

If the gentle chat and your offer of support doesn't work, then you can get into warnings and disciplinary action, but rarely is this necessary. Most people just need some help, or recognition, or flexibility (e.g. you agree different hours for the next couple of months), or rehabilitation, and it's sorted.

Legal advice

When you're working in a large corporation there is often a general counsel, or an in-house legal team, or an arrangement with an external law firm that also houses an employment lawyer. When you're in a smaller company, you find that either you are the resident employment law advisor, or it's a combination of you and some external help. This can come from a mentor with more experience, or it can come from an arrangement with a local law firm. The latter is the approach that I have taken in the past.

To find someone that is formally a specialist in employment law, go to the Law Society website and click on the area headed 'find a solicitor', type in 'employment law' and your postcode and then go meet a few. Ask them how they can help you. They may offer a retainer service, or a fee per service. It's a commercial decision that only you can make, but I've always found it useful to have someone 'on call'.

A less expensive alternative is to use the helpdesk of a more generic country-wide provider, where you pay a monthly subscription and have 24/7 phone access. And then there are some services that are free, including some Employee Advisory Resource services, CIPD if you are a member, and Citizens Advice.

The difference between talking to a lawyer or an HR mentor about an issue, is that the former will give you the letter of the law to follow, and often a choice to make, whereas the latter will give you the best practical way of resolving something. I now have grey hair, and years of experience, so I'm in a position where I will probably take risks and deal directly with an issue, trying to nip it in the bud. And that's because once both sides get lawyers involved, it is possible to see people becoming entrenched in positions which are difficult to break, and the only winners are the lawyers, who keep sending their invoices alongside their advice. Not all lawyers are like this. There are notable exceptions.

55

LinkedIn

Always worthy of a mention, LinkedIn is a go-to place for many HR and recruitment teams seeking information on an individual and wanting to find out who they know, to see a simple résumé, or sometimes to look at their qualifications and recommendations. I'm not going to make this an advert, LinkedIn has its downsides, but simply to say that if you work in HR, you should always make sure your profile is up to date and reasonably informative. When looking at other people's profiles, just be aware that sometimes they don't always stand up to scrutiny. Check out their claims rather than recruit purely based on their profile.

56

Mediation and Arbitration

A powerful, and probably underused, tool that should be in every HR Head's kit bag. Every so often in your working life you will be asked to help resolve a difficult situation that has arisen between two or more people. Sometimes a separate chat with both sides, finding a compromise, and bringing them back together, is all that is required. To achieve this, you have to listen hard and question why someone has reached a particular view, probing at the edges for any possibility of an alternate solution. Try not to threaten them, or their position, in a way that forces them to dig deeper into their trench; instead use words like 'perception' to express your feelings in a relaxed way. Help them see that there might be an alternative that can work for both sides, for the good of the organisation.

There will be times when the problem is deep-rooted, or where you personally know one of the parties too well. These are moments when employing a professional mediator can work a treat. An external third party, with no axe to grind, can often unlock issues in a way like no other.

If mediation fails, then pendulum arbitration can work a treat. In essence you create a panel of people who are not connected with either side, and ask them to hear both sides present their solution to the problem. You explain that the panel has to choose one solution only. I have seen both parties, seemingly entrenched in positions from which they had sworn never to budge, to present an amazing compromise to a panel, in the knowledge that they will have to live with whichever solution the panel picks. Indeed, in one case, both sides presented the same solution to the panel.

57

Mental Health Concerns

If you notice a change in someone's behaviour, enough to have concerns, it is always worth inviting them to go for a coffee and asking if they are okay. This simple question, asked with sincerity and time to listen to the response, can change someone's life.

Does your workplace have Mental Health First Aiders, Occupational Health, Private Medical Insurance or an Employee Advisory Resource Company? If it does then the person can be signposted to them. Offer to help them make the first step, maybe walking with them and introducing them to someone who can help. If yours is a small company and has none of these facilities then they can be referred to their own GP.

If the issue is affecting their work, then suggest they speak with their line manager. You can go with them if you and they want. If they are not okay, reaching out is so important, and letting them know that they are not alone, is key.

58

Mental Health Support

By guest author, and expert in this field, Natasha Gordon.

This chapter assumes you have the support of your management team or exec in building a mental health capability. It assumes they have recognised the key benefits, which include staff retention, increased engagement and productivity, decreased sickness absence, being an employer of choice, to name just a few.

Once agreed, then setting up an effective multi-choice system of support for staff in your organisation, with instant access options, is key to making the intervention a success. And it doesn't have to cost the earth. This case study covers the challenges, learnings and the options that were found to be effective and led to a direct impact on sickness absence figures. The following are elements to consider when starting up:

What to do first?

Before you launch straight into setting something up, you need to have an understanding of where the people in your organisation's heads are when it comes to mental health and wellbeing. Do they appreciate the impact mental ill health is having on the workforce, culture, productivity, engagement, retention and overall health of the organisation? In most places a small number of people will be completely committed to improving the support services available. They will have either experienced mental health issues personally, or they will have friends or family who have. Some won't quite 'get it', and will ask why this has to be made a special case, whilst others will believe that mental health has no place at work and should be left back at home. As mental health becomes more openly discussed in wider society, and more people realise the depth and breadth of the problem, this latter group is, thankfully, becoming smaller and less vocal, but there will always be a handful of naysayers, so it is important to listen to their reasons, engage with them, then use them as your measure of success later in the project.

Once you've spoken to a number of people, maybe run a small survey for staff, and made presentations, used feedback forums or focus groups, and published your project on the organisation's internal intranet or noticeboards, you can then create a mental health interest group. By meeting regularly, maybe over tea/coffee/cake (that you provide as a thank you), you can discuss ideas, create actions, assign owners, agree deadlines and make sure there are planned and structured outcomes that flow from the group.

In one organisation the initial announcement was made at a town hall meeting (for all staff), and those interested were asked to sign up after the meeting. Be ready for greater initial interest than you might expect.

Working Group

By getting all the interested people together for a meeting, you can discuss ideas and initiatives that you would like to instigate, as well as finding out what ideas the group have. Some will have a partner or a friend at a company that already runs mental health initiatives; others will have specific points they are passionate about that need to be considered. Go to the first meeting prepared. What training opportunities will you be able to make available (and do you have the budget)? What amount of time will volunteers be asked to give up? What outcomes (short, middle and longer term) do you ideally want? You will need to be prepared to change tack and for quite different ideas to emerge from the group discussions, but it is good to have a plan ready as a straw person to be knocked around. If you are considering the provision of training in mental health awareness, or MH First Aid, discuss this with the group, especially the likely numbers needed in each division or establishment, and how far the budget can stretch for the first intake.

Pilot Scheme

The first thing I did with the working group was to get approval for external training with Mental Health First Aid England (MHFA). You may find that advertising this programme as a pilot to your budget holders will ease their approval concerns. With our pilot, we asked members of the working group in the first instance if they would like to be in the first training cohort. We created a document, similar to a role profile, that outlined the expectations of the MHFA role, and a document for them all to sign confirming that any conversations would be confidential between them and the person they were helping. This gave credibility to what became the Mental Health Network.

We trained twelve people to be Mental Health First Aiders (MHFAers), and here lay our first challenge. Of the two trainers, one had an approach of focusing on sharing personal stories, and less data discussion, while the other focused on the data to show why this type of training was important, followed by tools to take away in approaching a conversation with an individual. One engaged their group completely, while the other fell flat. My first and perhaps most important tip would be to ensure that you have the right trainer for your audience, as these people will either get buy-in, or buy-out will occur as word of mouth spreads fast.

Once the first rounds of training were complete, the results of the pilot programme were communicated to the rest of the organisation. This led to more people expressing an interest, and before we knew it, we had sufficient volunteers to cover illness and provide a diverse mix of people that employees could choose between when seeking support. We added some regular communications on mental health and wellbeing, signs and symptoms and line manager responsibility to start the buy-in and engagement process on a broader scale. We made use of world mental health awareness day and kept the group meeting regularly to share feedback and make amendments as necessary.

Training and Confidentiality

Depending on the pace of pick-up and interest received after launch, a number of additional people will want to have the same MHFA training. In your working group meetings, you will already have decided how to manage this, but be sure to keep these guidelines under review, as it is key to maintaining interest and engagement at this early stage. Creating a waiting list for future training dates, providing a newsletter, publishing a FAQ sheet and sharing resources and insights all help to keep the group motivated.

It is important to report back to your exec or management team on outcomes of the pilot and its effectiveness. When it comes to mental health and wellbeing and the confidentialities surrounding it, gathering data can feel like a minefield. You will have the role profile and confidentiality forms at hand to show, but what also worked well to get our pilot approved for full launch was sourcing quantitative data. We did this by keeping an anonymous tracker. MHFAers told us how many conversations they had had, key themes that came up and the gender of the people they were supporting (any more details and people start to worry about whether they can be identified). We could then plainly see how much the network was being used and what themes might need more communications and support from the group. We also gathered and analysed sickness data, which would become a helpful success measure over the first two years.

Once you have launched and up to twelve months

Keep the communications and momentum up as this is where you get your qualitative data: culture change, feedback, people who weren't supportive to begin with, but now are, etc. It is an interesting time and one where you might start to see some real changes. Keep tracking your sickness data: is mental ill health a reason for absence? If not, get it added. Does that change the options people are selecting? Make some decisions around any anonymous options available for absences. Is there a correlation between the MHFAer conversations tracker and sickness absence?

Twelve months onwards

It's important that you don't allow all your hard work to fade away. Having reported back to the management team on the use of the programme, it is also important to remind the employees of the changes that have been made and to give them an idea of how you will build on your success.

A good option is to create a Wellness Action Plan (the mind.org website has some great examples), which can lead to constructive and helpful conversations between employees and their line managers and HR, and most significantly, asking your MH network if anyone would be interested in sharing their personal experiences with the rest of the organisation. You have to time this right by checking in on where the culture has moved to. Are they ready to hear this? This could sound melodramatic, but with mental ill health being so common, hearing a personal account can stir up employee experiences that they may not have been able to get help with yet. Sensitivity and thorough thinking through are needed here.

If you can encourage a number of people to come to come forward to share their stories, either at an all-staff meeting, or by writing an account for the intranet, you will start to open up the conversation for all. This is not something that can be done anonymously; it needs a few courageous people to talk about their experiences and be named. Once this happens you should be ready for another wave of volunteers, and more people offering to tell their story. By doing so, you start to see a shift in culture, from MH being hidden and stigmatised, to being talked about openly and supportively. The shift in gear, culture, support, gratitude and absence figures can be quite remarkable.

At around this stage ask your directors if they would like to attend the training. Most will, and then some will share their stories, at which point you know you are finally embedding mental health awareness and you can start thinking about other aspects of wellbeing.

What next?

The direction that you take will depend on the type and nature of organisation. But you can expect a drop in absence rates and a much more caring environment in which MH is not a stigma or hidden, but openly discussed and supported. By introducing directors and senior managers into the mix, and by creating a new preventative network, you can start to introduce best practice. You can create a pathway with your support resources: EAP, OH, PMI, Gym, HR, etc, to clarify to the organisation how much support is available, where to go for help, and how to avoid issues like stress and anxiety in the first place.

59

Mentoring

A lot of people are put off mentoring because they automatically think about big programmes that they have to commit to, speed dating to find a match, confidentiality contracts and time-consuming visits to see strangers. Well, I have another view.

For me mentoring is about the chance to give something back to the next generation of Human Resources folk and, at the same time, learn from them about all the changes going on in the profession from their perspective. It's about meeting up on an irregular basis when a crunch decision is needed and exploring all the avenues available. Confidentiality is a given: it doesn't need a contract, especially in the HR world.

My most enjoyable mentoring sessions are often with people I have previously line-managed. I know them well, they know me well, and yet we are no longer in a direct working relationship, so they and I can say what is needed. I also enjoy being referred by someone to provide help or support to a new HRD or similar. More often than not, my job is to listen and then confirm that the course of action they are considering is the right one, a confidence booster. But sometimes it can be to say 'and have you thought of any other alternatives' when it's clear they are heading in the wrong direction.

Many mentoring meetings focus on the pros and cons of applying for a new job. Sometimes it's about how to deal with a difficult relationship with a line manager; sometimes it's about being a line manager for the first time. Occasionally, it's about dissecting a failed application or interview and learning from it, or it's about another issue like illness or broken relationships (but those are rare in comparison to the work-related nature of mentoring).

I added up the number of people I 'mentor'. Currently, it's nearly fifty people. 'Mentor' is in inverted commas, because I haven't seen the majority for six to twelve months. They get in touch with me when they have a need, and I just prompt them with the occasional catch-up message in the meantime. I will also add at this point that I too am mentored by nearly fifty people, because every time I meet them, I learn something new about the world, about me or about them, and I come away feeling better than before I started.

If you don't have a mentor, then go get some! The best place to start is usually a previous tutor or line manager, or someone you respect in a more senior role than yours. Don't ask them to be your mentor; allow it to happen over time. Instead, ask them if they are free for a coffee or lunch (at your expense), as you would like to ask their advice. Things will either progress from there, or you'll need to try someone else, but nine times out of ten you'll be meeting up with them again and things will flourish. Just remember to send a note of thanks after the encounter that includes something you're now doing differently. And there are no rules about how many mentors you can have.

If you don't mentor people, then go start! If you see someone you used to work with or maybe line managed, who is struggling with a job or an issue, or who is working in another department and is showing promise, then offer to have a chat over coffee. Listen to what they are doing and saying, and as the conversation develops you will naturally fall into a mentoring relationship. The first person I mentored was a new graduate who looked completely lost in the world of work. I still catch-up with him these days, although he's now a COO!

(Reverse) Mentoring

Reverse mentoring is a term that is starting to be used in the work setting to describe the opportunity to help someone in a senior role understand the work, or life, of a less experienced employee, or someone from a different generation.

A powerful example I saw in action was a director who really didn't understand the need to take race discrimination seriously. She spent just ninety minutes with a young black guy, learning all about the issues he faced both at work and in the wider world, and immediately came back and signed up to a plan of meaningful action.

Personally, I have found I am forever benefitting from reverse mentoring, just by mentoring a range of people. I get numerous insights into the issues that affect them, see the world from their perspective, and occasionally succeed in helping them either see a light, realise just what they are capable of, and/or find a way around a perceived obstacle. Mentoring doesn't need to be through a scheme, it can just be the natural extension of a few chats over tea or coffee.

Mentoring Schemes

Mentoring schemes in themselves can be slow and cumbersome as a way forward, and often involve an arduous set-up and much lost time as people develop their confidence in each other after signing countless waiver and disclaimer forms. If you enter a scheme to be a mentor or a mentee, then make sure you benefit from the training sessions that they run, some of which can be helpful, covering things like non-directive coaching and boundaries.

The main reason to seek out a mentor is to bounce ideas off someone who is not a part of your current team or line management. You can think issues through (normally around work and career, but inevitably home and family play a part) in a confidential space with someone you respect.

The best mentors are already in your network. They are previous line managers, senior colleagues, tutors, etc. Don't start by asking them to be your mentor, as that can sound a bit scary. Instead, just ask if you could buy them a coffee/lunch as you would respect their advice on something and then see how it works out. Having several mentors, for different circumstances, can also be a good thing.

62 |

Mergers

When organisations listed on the stock exchange plan a merger, the press often report it before employee announcements can be made, either due to leaks from the negotiating teams, or from the big investors who have been consulted. A merger is often a misnomer: the reality is that one organisation acquires the other, and the CEO of the new combined organisation sets the tone and culture and shape of the new venture.

Call me a cynic, but I have yet to see a merger where the power of the new entity combined is more than the sum of the two added together. And the reason for this is simple. As soon as the announcements appear in the press, a large number of projects and programmes are frozen, awaiting decisions on what the new company's priorities are going to be. Equally, many people become less efficient and productive, wanting to talk to others about the possibilities, about whether their job will survive, whether their work location will move. In short, it's an unsettling process for everyone, and that period of unsettled status lasts throughout the period of inevitable restructuring that follows the announcement. Much time is also lost awaiting the due diligence to be completed, the completion of the mergers and acquisitions authorities review, and the complexities of shareholder votes.

My advice is to clear the decks and be ready to see your work load double, and your chances of a proper holiday disappear for the next six to twelve months.

There is no rule book or play book for a perfect merger, it doesn't exist. Usually, a big consulting firm is given the task of re-engineering the workforce and the HR teams become the pawns, asked for loads of data and then later asked to implement impossible new structures. Where you do get the opportunity to join working teams or project groups, grab them, and use every opportunity to influence the decision-making, so that life is as dignified and reasonable as possible for the people in your company. Have a look at sections in this book on change, communication and redundancy.

Even if you struggle to get to the table and find that consultants are dictating the changes, it is still worth putting time and effort into communications. Make sure all staff receive regular updates; that there are open channels for people to ask questions; that rumours are heard and responded to, and not allowed to fester. Whole books have been written about mergers; this is just a short section to highlight that when presented with a merger or acquisition, an early task is to find a mentor who has been through this before, and to start reading up the many works on making a success of M&A.

Metrics and Dashboards

In many larger companies, and increasingly in smaller ones, there is a demand for measures of output from each division. It's always been the case in sales-driven organisations, the need to know what customers are demanding, what is selling well, what is being held up, profit margins, etc.

HR teams are routinely asked to provide data such as turnover, time to hire to fill vacancies, training days attended, holidays accrued and sickness absence rates. Even if you are not asked for these on a regular basis, you should either have access through your HR System, or someone in your team who knows how to collate the data in a timely way. Since all data takes time to produce (either by the individual having to respond, or the team member collating and checking), it is important to review what is collected and what value it holds. I have stopped several data metrics, and reduced the subsequent displays on dashboards, when I have discovered that – literally – no one was using them. Equally, I have introduced relevant metrics when either I have perceived there is a potential problem, or it has been raised by a line manager. Try not to allow movements in trend lines to be overly interpreted by others. Used sensibly as an early warning indication of issues requiring further investigation, they are fine.

Monthly Reports

Some organisations have formed a bad habit that has been compounded over many, many years. They demand weekly, or monthly, reports that feature a whole string of subheadings that have to be completed and then moved up the line. Given that they take time out of the organisation when people could be being more productive, are they actually serving a purpose? If you've arrived in a new role and you're being asked for a report, ask where it goes, what it is used for, and for some evidence that it is worth bothering with. Unfortunately, too many people slavishly complete their reports, wasting significant time in doing so, aggregate them, and pass them up the line. Personally, I would rather spend time with the team asking what's going well, and where the issues are, rather than asking them to fill out pro-forma report sheets.

A fair test of the value of a report is, therefore, to send exactly the same report this month that you sent last month. And repeat. If no one ever challenges you, then you know it is not serving any real purpose. If they do spot what you're up to, apologise, explaining that you accidently sent the old one, and that the up-to-date version will follow. At one major company I worked for I encouraged other peers to do the same. After three months we confessed to the SVP. And that was the last report we ever had to do, until a new SVP arrived, and we were sent back to square one! If your reports are easy to produce because everything is run by the ERP system, or some other software, then check it is validated data that is being sent: sometimes the coding is awry and you can end up submitting worthless data without realising it.

65

Negotiation

One of the biggest hurdles to negotiation, whether it be between two people, or two sets of people, is a lack of understanding of the issues as seen by the other party. I'm regularly approached by employees who are struggling to instigate a change to their job, or managers who are struggling to see improvements from their staff. And often the best thing to do is get them to switch positions and see the problem from the other perspective.

In some cases, this can be dramatically improved by sitting in the other person's chair. Many times, I have taken someone who is struggling with their boss and asked them to sit in their boss's chair (when they are away from the office, of course), and I have then role-played with them. I ask a question about time off, a pay rise, the chances of a re-grading or promotion, and persuade them to role-play as their boss. Just that simple act opens their eyes and they change their approach. They see that they have to think about the wider implications of the change on the department, and that there needs to be a justification for their change, or a clear benefit for the organisation that can be explained by their boss to the next person up the corporate tree if needed.

Having truly understood both sides of the issue, the next thing is to research solutions already out there. This is where the internet earns its keep. Whatever issue you need to negotiate, someone has been there before and left a trail for you to find and learn from.

You now have a refined proposition: you have examples of how it has worked elsewhere and what the benefits of the change are to the other party. Now you need to decide on your backstop. In other words, what is the least that you will settle on, what would be acceptable, and what would feel great? If you have thought through the advantages from the other party's perspective, then you may even reach the best possible place in negotiation. There have been many times when my response has been 'yes' to a well-argued case. Think through how you will present it, how you will help the other party understand what the issue is, why things need to change and what your proposal is. Keep it as basic as you can. If you can achieve the in-principle agreement for change, then the details can follow later.

If you think about all this, then you'll realise that what you need are Advanced Sales Skills, which is often a cheaper training programme to attend than Advanced Negotiation Skills.

When negotiating between two groups, classically in HR we represent the management view and work with the trade union or employee representatives. The above still applies, but the key now is to ensure that everyone in your team fully understands your position and what you will and won't give way on. I've been in situations where I have prepared with my team and still been surprised by either an offer, or a request, from the other side. The best way to deal with this is to withdraw, discuss amongst the team, seek a view from the CEO if needed, and then re-enter the room to progress the meeting.

Pride is often an issue. Both sides need to be able to show their constituents that they have achieved something and made progress. Management negotiation teams that don't understand this, and believe that they have to 'win', inevitably lose in the long term. And because pride exists even within the negotiating team, sometimes the only way to make a breakthrough is for the two leaders from each side to have a chat during a break and agree a way forward once back in the room.

In most circumstances it is getting an agreement in principle that is most difficult, with the detail taking the most time. I've learned that the best way to get all the tricky issues resolved is for both sides to appoint small teams to work them through and then come back to the main negotiating team with a list of items that need to be resolved. Often these can be traded, so that both sides can leave feeling they have made progress.

Communications, as ever, are key. The best negotiators can be caught out by leaks from the negotiating team to people outside (sometimes the press, who can be persistent in wanting to get a scoop). To resolve this, the only way is to ensure that everyone on both sides understands how high the stakes are, and how important it is that everything is kept confidential, and then to have agreements between both parties about which statements are released to other employees and/or the media and at what times as the talks progress.

Some of my best moments at work have been in negotiation, whether with a trade union, an executive committee or resolving a dispute between a manager and employee. Handled with common sense, humility and recognising the need to preserve the dignity and pride of both parties makes it easier than most would imagine.

66

Networking

Events where you sign up, attend a hotel somewhere, enter a room, get a name badge and then have to chat to people aren't everyone's cup of tea, and can be quite traumatic, especially for introverts. And yet networking can be very simple.

You have a network of people you went to school with, another network if you went to college or university, a network at places you have worked and yet another at the school gate or club or church or whatever activity you are involved in.

Find any of those people that you haven't spoken to in a while, who might be relevant to your current role, in places like Facebook and LinkedIn. Send them a note such as 'Hi, it's a while since we last spoke, how are you doing?' Some won't answer, but some will. Offer to buy them a tea or coffee near where they work or live and arrange a chat.

If it's someone you respect and admire, then don't scare them off by asking them to be a mentor, instead say something like 'I'm thinking about this, do you have any advice?' Don't overstay your welcome; follow up later with a message saying how valuable the chat was and ask if a repeat would be possible in three to six months' time. Repeat a few times and you will soon have a useful network!

67

New Leader Assimilation

It can be tricky for a senior manager or director to arrive in an organisation from the outside world (or in a big company, from another division), and get up to speed quickly as the leader of an established group. One Hundred Day Plans play their part, as does a proper induction, or the opportunity to work with teams and discover what they are doing, but none of them address the concerns and issues that the current team have.

One of the reasons why it is tricky, is that the division will have heard rumours about the new manager or director, picked up gossip from the rumour mill, and will often lack trust or understanding.

As a means of speeding up the process of assimilation, the process I describe here was used when Glaxo merged with Wellcome, a period of time when groups of employees from one company suddenly discovered that they had a new boss from the other partner in the merger. They were concerned about their future, having invested much in their previous leader, and had heard reports from colleagues about what the new person was like.

The process ran as follows: a neutral facilitator from a different division or organisation invited the group of people about to be led by the new leader into a workshop, and met just with them for the morning. By the end of that time a series of flip charts was completed, detailing what they already knew about their new leader, their hope and expectations for the coming months, their strengths and weaknesses as a team and any perceived opportunities or threats. Once happy with the lists, the team was then sent for a break, whilst the facilitator invited the new leader into the room, together with their HR business partner, to review the flip charts.

The facilitator worked with the leader and HRBP to understand the issues and concerns and what had been heard during the session. Following a few minutes to prepare notes, the team were brought back in and invited to listen to their new leader. After some trial runs, it was considered best for the leader to describe a bit about their career and achievements to date, and disclose a little about their families, their hobbies and interests to help them come over as a real human with a life outside of work. They would then address the issues raised, often using the flip charts as prompts to give opinions, push back on false rumours and then assign initial priorities for the coming months. And if they didn't know an answer, we always insisted that they said so, and that they would look at the issue over the coming weeks and report back. Once the leader had given an initial response, a formal question and answer session followed, and then a more informal chance to chat with smaller groups over tea/coffee.

We were a science organisation, and so we ran some control experiments, looking at the speed with which teams assimilated under a new leader both with, and without, the programme. It helped massively, in whatever way it was measured, and went on to be used extensively in the R&D division, right up until the next merger, where the new Chief People Officer didn't like the idea, and it was squashed!

68

Offshoring

This section is written by Sarah Collins, who has much greater experience of this than I do.

Offshoring is seen as a way of reducing one of the most significant costs on the profit and loss account, staffing; albeit some companies are wary, due to the bad press that some early overseas call centres had.

When I was given the task of offshoring a section of the organisation, I started by hiring a project manager with specific experience on a fixed-term contract. This was essential, as all my normal HR work just continued to pile up. HR people are all too good at trying to make do and mend, whilst other departments make use of experienced support.

Definition of the drivers and success criteria

Early on it was clear that the exec team had different views of what this offshoring project meant, and some had preconceived ideas. By starting with the success criteria, we managed to get everything on the table and make considered joint decisions about what our organisation needed, and why each was essential, or desirable. The success criteria were key when we had wobbles along the way, to check that what we were doing still met our goals.

Once drafted, the success criteria need to be critically evaluated to make sure it's the right thing to do as an organisation, that the timing is right, and that it does not deflect from other key strategic projects. For us there were other critical projects in parallel, but this discussion flushed out how we would manage it and who would be able to help and when.

Define which functions will have resources in the new location

This requires a debate at exec level, and needs to be put into the perspective of what is right for the business, rather than what is right for each senior leader's division. The types of roles should be clarified, including whether they will be made up of new headcount (organisational growth) or existing headcount. If the latter, then will that occur through natural attrition or relocation/ redundancy? If you are not on the exec team yourself, make sure you have a key sponsor who is (not necessarily your boss) and that they are fully engaged with the project, and can help challenge people who waver.

Investigation, desk and location research

We came up with a shortlist of locations based on desk research, and found data about government-run programmes to encourage overseas organisations to move to their country via national and local government offices. Other key data about education of potential employees, political volatility, corruption, costs of living, unemployment levels, transportation into and within the country, and employment law followed. Having identified companies who had already moved to these markets, we called them and talked to them. They were candid about their experiences and this saved a lot of time.

We proceeded to get board-level approval for the three locations that we would visit and started to develop in-depth profiles. During our visits we met with Chambers of Commerce, local mayoral offices and legal firms, and we went to see what sort of offices would be available.

We met with recruitment companies and, armed with job descriptions, discussed the full cost of hiring these roles (pay, benefit, tax, etc) and the ease of hiring them. This was key to our decision-making and ruled out several possibilities, as we found that the markets had overheated and finding staff would have been a challenge.

Communication

The project was viewed with scepticism by some existing staff, even though this was a growth story, and no jobs in current locations were lost. We had to be clear and consistent in our messages, and be open about the progress of the project as much as we could. We held smaller group Q&A sessions to give people the opportunity to discuss their hopes and concerns.

We found it important to keep key staff engaged with the project. Having them involved in hiring new staff helped in creating international relationships, and in some cases led to mentoring opportunities, as well as a chance to adopt a new holiday destination.

Implementation

Early on we knew we needed lawyers for both commercial and employment purposes. We sought a partner who could cover both angles, and had a track record of being capable of providing both theoretical, but perhaps more importantly, practical advice. This saved time and money as a result.

Office location search and contracting was a sub-project in its own right. Having said that, we were relatively lucky and found an empty office right in the centre of the town we had chosen, with good transport links, and a landlord who had several town centre properties, providing us with future opportunities for growth. The office fit-out was the real challenge. The project manager and I were both female and blonde, and for the first time in this project, this seemed to be a problem. After weeks of frustration, being unable to make headway in sourcing office materials and furniture, and negotiating prices for fit-out, we asked a local country manager we were interviewing why we were struggling. His response was, that unless we could shout and swear in Romanian, we would never succeed in this area! We hired someone who could do both, and the project moved forward in leaps and bounds. Office design and layout was, of course, in line with both our budget and our overall company culture.

In setting up the infrastructure we needed contracts of employment, a payroll arrangement, a financial and legal entity, and tax and legal registrations with Government bodies. (These are essential for all of the obvious reasons, but watch out for the relationship between some of these items and being able to secure an office and hire your first staff, and run a test payroll.) We found that the partnering company were not as quick as they had told us, and that rules about transferring money had delays built into them, all of which would have led to delays in paying staff, and potentially breaking the law as a result, if we had not run the pilot.

Regarding hiring, we had identified key roles, selected our recruitment partners and formed an understanding of the most successful recruitment routes in the local market. We discovered that the appointment of the country manager was key. (The person has to be local and must be hired as soon as possible, the challenge being their notice period from the current job will be the longest out of all staff. Be clear what autonomy they will have, and what will be decided by Head Office.) We rejected candidates who told us they ignored what Head Office wanted, and did what they wanted. When we found the right candidate, it was critical that they met all the key senior people so they could buy into the organisation, culture and team as quickly as possible.

Press recruitment agencies hard to evidence how they will prioritise your roles over other projects. One of our agencies promised us the world, but delivered little, as they were sending all the best candidates to other local companies. Look at career fairs, link up with universities and talk to the mayor and their team about where to hire from. We did exceptionally well by having an employee referral programme in place which paid more than other companies, but cost us one-tenth of the price of an agency.

Plans for onboarding and employee benefits to attract and retain staff also had to be made early on. The first fifty staff were onboarded via the UK and other EU offices. This was seen as attractive by the new hires and was easier in the early days when we were still trying to finish the office fit-out in the new location. We chose to see employee benefits as a jar of sweets: we gave some out in the first year and allowed staff to negotiate future enhancements in subsequent years. The staff appreciated this and we managed the costs appropriately.

Go Live

When new hires are on board and the office is operational, ensure there is a rota of key people to visit the office from HQ and to make the new hires feel they have joined the right company. Spend time listening to them. We got some basic things wrong about coffee provision and cup clearing in the early days that caused small upsets, but because we talked to staff openly, we were quick to pick it up and sort it out. Not everything can be done on, or for, day one, but having a plan to keep on top of delivering everything else was necessary before other projects took over was equally important.

Celebrate!

We had a party and invited the local mayor and the press, and made a big event of it with the board in attendance too. It helped us announce we had arrived in the market, and assisted with our future recruitment.

(The) Organisation

One of the pleasures of working in HR is that you will regularly be turned to in a management team, exec or board meeting and asked 'What do the employees think?' It can be about any situation or issue at any time, and this is when you truly realise the annual employee survey doesn't help at all. You and I know there is rarely a single generic answer to a question like this. As with politics and all other aspects of life, the more employees you have, the more views there will be on any particular subject, unless, of course, there has just been a ballot with 100% backing. But even then, do you *really* know the motivation behind each vote?

When asked such a question, the important thing is that you have enough information to hand to give a fair summary of the group's hopes and concerns. To be able to do that you need to spend time away from your desk or HR office, chatting to different groups of people and listening to them, and you need to make space in your diary to do this regularly.

The easiest starting point is to take breaks seriously. When you go to fetch a drink, stand and chat to the people at the coffee machine, or sit with people that are not in your team. In a bigger organisation, go to a break room in another building. If you don't know the people, introduce yourself and ask if it's okay to join them; let them know that you're interested in any ideas they have to improve the environment (for example), and before long you'll move on to important issues. If you do take action on something, make sure they know, and your reputation will develop.

Lunchtimes are an excellent opportunity for interaction, and are lost to so many who insist they have too much to do and eat sandwiches at their desks. Thirty or forty minutes spent eating lunch with people who aren't in your immediate team can be a great way to understand the views and feelings of others, or just to catch up on the gossip.

Some of the people who really know what is going on are all too easily forgotten. When you get a chance, have a chat with your security officers, your cleaners, your receptionists, your post handlers, your IT contractors (or helpdesk operators), your travel team and your catering team. These people are often in early, or are still around in the evening. They are a key part of your team and yet many people will hardly ever acknowledge them, let alone talk to them. Ask them about their job, ask them about any changes that could make things easier for them, ask them who they enjoy working with. Offer them a coffee and cake, get to know them not just for ten minutes, but pop back a week later and ask again, and build a relationship. You never know where it will take you. In my case I have discovered all sorts of things, and I have helped a good number into new and different roles: many had become stuck in their current role but had the ability to do so much more.

Depending on the type of organisation you work in, another group of people that have a good insight into the organisation are the EAs and the PAs. You can learn so much from this group, as they are the interface between the senior leaders and the divisions or departments. They will know what is cooking, what the issues of the moment are, and have a good idea of what needs to change. Getting to know them, and helping them with their issues, will also help you in the long run, for example, when you need a real favour to get into a packed director's diary! At larger organisations I have run lunchtime get-togethers for the PAs, providing a free lunch, and in return received help with the introduction of new policies, and ironing out the edges of existing ones, as well as picking up rumours at an early stage.

On the subject of free food, I've personally also learned a lot from birthday breakfast meetings (people from all levels with a birthday that week or month, are invited for croissant, fruit, cereals and tea/coffee and a chat), buffet lunches to celebrate a project milestone, celebrations for significant service, and awards nights (a chance to celebrate the best people and teams, all nominated from within).

If you do have employee councils, or staff committees, or joint meetings with the trade unions, it is fine to delegate the running of these to your team members, but you need to attend, not just to answer tough questions, but also to be able to judge the mood of the representatives about a range of subjects. Note down significant things that are said and quote these at meetings with senior leaders that you then attend. Once you have built a relationship with them, start testing ideas for change together. Let them know you want their first thoughts in confidence, and that nothing is for certain, it's still at an early stage. By treating them as adults, you get a return on your investment. In my case I averted several errors by trying things out with the trade union team and then rapidly modifying them as a consequence.

As you start to engage more and more with the various people in your organisation, don't forget the power of communication. When you realise an issue needs fixing, sort it out and then let everyone know about the changes that you are making and acknowledge the source. What is wrong, for example, in giving praise to the trade union, or to a staff committee, if they have raised an issue and you have made a change as a consequence? By acknowledging their role in the process, more people will take the opportunity to put forward their own views and your organisation can only grow stronger as a result.

70 |

Outplacement

Outplacement is the term used to help someone transition from a job from which they are (usually) being made redundant. The great thing about it is that third-party counsellors work with you to establish what you want to do (a career change is common) and make sure all the basics are in place: current job search techniques, improved CV and cover note, networking tips, research tips, how to work with agencies and interview techniques, to name just a few. At its simplest, outplacement is not expensive, and generates a huge amount of goodwill, often for the family members of the affected person, who see that the company is providing ongoing practical support after the redundancy. At its best, it is an uplifting service that helps encourage people to regain their confidence, and sometimes move into a brand new career.

To engage with an outplacement firm, search for recommendations online and call a couple, comparing prices and ideas of what they can offer your colleagues. Some offer a fixed package, others a modular system, where the person chooses the aspects most valuable to them. One-to-one consultancy usually features, plus you can pay more for people to have complete individual support, or less by attending group seminars. The latter can be beneficial, as it gives people the chance to meet with others also recently made redundant and share experiences.

71

Outsourcing

Many organisations now outsource their non-core activities on the grounds that they want to concentrate on their mainstream activity or to reduce costs. For example, a pharmaceutical firm might outsource a specialist cleaner to move between premises with the best trained people using the best equipment, or a caterer might benefit from bulk-buying ingredients. The most common functions that are outsourced are cleaning, catering and security services, sometimes to specialists in each field, other times to one complete facilities provider. Other outsourced providers that I have worked with in HR terms have covered pensions, payroll and recruitment. The most positive experiences I have had have been with family-run companies with a real pride in their work that operated in a limited geographic area. My experiences with nationwide providers have mostly been poor.

If you receive complaints about someone who works for an outsourced company (often those who come into direct contact with your staff, such as security, catering, or IT), you need to raise this with whoever runs the contract in your organisation and/or the line manager. Explain that it has the potential to bring the organisation into disrepute and needs to be rectified quickly. Ensure that they have the evidence, as the person being complained about may be unaware of the impact they have had or are having.

The matter should then be dealt with under the contractor's procedures, not yours, and their disciplinary code, or as a welfare issue if there are extenuating circumstances (e.g. illness or medication that may have had an impact). Their HR team should be involved, not you. Often an outsourcing organisation will move such a person to another site because they won't want to lose your business. From the affected person's perspective, they then get a chance to adjust and make amends.

72

Pay in HR

Pay rates for HR roles and job titles vary depending upon location, sector and the respect that HR has in the organisation. At the lowest pay rates, we usually find the apprentice HR group, their wages being enhanced by training and development at college, with a qualification as the prize at the end. Administrators and assistant roles come next, again mostly enhanced by training opportunities. After that the only way you can really work out what someone does for their title is to ask them. I've seen people moving from Head of HR to HR Business Partner and get a pay rise along with more responsibility, and I have learned not to assume that an HR Advisor in one place is equivalent to an HR Advisor in another.

Once you have found a job that you enjoy, remind yourself that it is quite a special thing, so before you leave for more pay elsewhere, it might be worth fighting for, especially since (we assume) your employer won't want to lose you.

Use a search engine to find salaries for your job title, adverts with pay, LinkedIn jobs and salary survey sites (search for 'salary checker'). Talk to agencies or search consultants. Look at pay ranges in local universities and local government. Keep a spreadsheet with all the data and use it to provide an average and a range. Separately, put together a table showing your take home pay (after deductions), and what is spent on the big items like commuting and rent.

Think about the structure of the organisation and your skills, and see if you can identify an opportunity that would give your boss the excuse to move or promote you and give you a pay rise. Take the data to your line manager and explain that you love what you do, but you can't afford to stay. Provide some evidence to support your claim, and explain that you're thinking about leaving. If nothing happens then you won't feel bad about resigning at a later date, or about asking for time off for interviews.

73

Pay Grades

Grading systems can be found in many organisations. As an incoming head of HR, you will often hear about how awful the system is, and how much it needs to be changed. The difficulty is that there is no perfect grading system in existence anywhere, nor has there ever been. The only perfect systems exist where there is one employee in the company. Any more and there will always be issues. Sometimes it is better to keep the current system rather than replace it, and instead consult widely, making appropriate small changes for improvement. Given that most people will have a feeling of their relative status based on the current system, and will understand it, this is often easier than trying to introduce a whole new language around pay.

When used well, grading systems can help give people in the organisation a clear idea about where they can aim, and what remuneration they will receive, and can be used to ensure everyone is fairly rewarded. Job evaluation is often used as a technique to 'score' one role in comparison to others. Some agencies make their money out of providing complex systems where you input variables (experience, qualifications, responsibility, budget levels) and produce a points-based grading result. These can help with the basics of ensuring parity and fairness, but none of them cope well with changing market forces. To resolve these, some companies offer a premium on top of the normal salary range for a grade to compensate for market scarcity. This premium rate can increase or decrease as the market moves. In the case of IT, for example, it may be that a new development language emerges and you have to pay a premium for a few years until the market corrects itself, usually when the colleges kick into gear and provide the appropriate training.

74

Perception

'Perception is a simple word that has helped me tremendously throughout my working life. I have learned the hard way that if you challenge someone head-on with a comment or a response, that they can become defensive, and instead of responding to the feedback, will entrench themselves in their position, or fight back in some other way.

By instead saying to someone that there is a *perception* that they have a particular trait, for example that they are dismissive of junior staff, you are not saying that you believe this to be true, purely that the perception has been created and needs to be addressed.

Let's look at an example of this in use. Several members of a team have said that they find the style of their manager to be bullying. This is not something you can ignore. Discretely asking other members of the team confirms that some members believe the manager is too direct and insufficiently consultative, but others reference the direct style as refreshing, and describe the manager as someone who likes to get things done, rather than talk about them. Rather than confronting the manager by telling him that he has been accused of bullying by team members, an alternative is to explain that the perception of some members is that he is too direct, and that he needs to spend a little more time explaining why he is doing things, consulting and discussing options with team members where appropriate.

Clearly if there is a formal accusation of bullying backed by concrete evidence, then it might not be possible to use this route, and you may need to suspend the person pending investigation. Bullying is a difficult area to deal with: one woman's bully can be another woman's no-nonsense decisive leader. Just look at world leaders for examples.

75

PLC versus PE

Working for a Public Limited Company is quite a different experience to working for a Private Equity backed company. In the plc a regular objective is for the company to make sufficient money on sale of goods or services to reward shareholders with increasing dividends (they own shares on the understanding that they will get a dividend that is at worst equal to inflation, and hopefully a few points ahead of inflation).

Shareholders understand that the company needs to retain, or hold back, some of its profits each year to invest in new programmes or projects that will reap money in the future. They expect some of those projects to fail, but that overall, they will earn more money every year from their dividends and, in time, see the value of the shares increase as well, to reflect the growth and size of the organisation.

Shareholders channel all their energy through the board, the CEO and the CFO, via representative groups, or funds that hold numerous clients' investments on their behalf. Working for a plc you will rarely meet shareholders. They will be in the background, and will occasionally show interest in the Remuneration Committee report into senior salaries and share options, that you will probably help prepare. Whilst the shareholders remain in the background, you will feel the pressure from your executive through objectives that are often published and defended at the annual meeting.

Meanwhile, in a private equity house, cash is king. They have chosen to invest in your company and want to get it to a point where it can be either sold to another company (a trade sale) or floated on the stock exchange (often called an IPO, an initial public offering). Typically, this occurs around five years after the initial investment, but can span from three to seven years. There are many variants, but these are the big ones.

PE houses invest in a range of companies and understand that some will fail, but that they will still make more money than they invest, when the good ones are sold. At separate steps of building a company up the investors will add additional funds, often called series A, series B funding rounds, etc. Because cash is king, if they feel that something is going wrong, they take control of the company. Often there is only a small number of large shareholders, who will visit the company regularly, and may want to meet with you and get opinions on how things are working out. They can be ruthless in replacing executives, selling assets, and closing down ventures they feel have no real chance of making them money. They want to know that the senior team have 'skin in the game', and they do this by giving them significant share options, and/or requiring them to invest their own cash in the business. The idea is that the stakes are high, but so are the potential rewards. Many also include all staff in their share schemes, and sometimes can be quite generous with remuneration packages, and will remain hands-off, if all is going well.

76

Presentations

The first presentations that I gave were awful. I made so many errors. I was unprepared and way too nervous. People who have seen me present in more recent years, to a thousand or more people at a CIPD conference, will find that difficult to believe, but hopefully you can also find your voice and style, and succeed with some training and practice. What surprises me is how many senior people have never sought feedback, and plough on making the same errors, wasting people's time, or annoying them.

Whenever I'm asked to give a presentation or a talk about a subject, I always ask the same questions. Can you tell me who has been (or will be) invited, who has accepted so far, and what roles do they play? What do you expect the audience to learn from me by presenting to them? What is the likely size of the audience? Will it take place in a small or medium-sized room, a theatre, or streamed online? What level of understanding of the topic do the audience have? Can I have a brief chat to some of the intended audience?

If you are being asked to present to your organisation's town hall (all staff) meeting, or the exec team or Remuneration Committee (RemCo), then you won't need to ask many of these questions, but if it is an outside organisation then the questions will be key to your success.

For a very small group, such as RemCo, it is often best to avoid the use of PowerPoint or Keynote, and instead prepare a deck of slides that you can submit with the papers. That way the members have a chance to read through the data first and use their time at the meeting more productively, to challenge your data, your assumptions, and come to a decision about how they want to proceed.

For a larger group, you may want to use a small number of slides. On the assumption that you have attended the training course Presentations 101 , the old mantra of tell them what you're going to tell them, tell them, and then tell them what you have told them, still works wonders. The main thing is to severely limit the number of bullet points on each slide. These are the key messages that you want to get across; they are not your crib sheet to either read from, or remind you what you should be saying. If you can replace words with diagrams, simple graphs or pictures, then even better. With simplicity comes the chance that people will hear what you have to say and remember the key points. If you are told at the beginning that you only have fifteen minutes, think about presenting for half that time and then taking questions and answers (it's often during the Q&A that people really start to understand what you're actually saying).

When presenting to employees on a new bonus scheme, pension scheme or share option scheme, remember that your knowledge is already way ahead of most of the audience's, so go back to basics and build up slowly, checking for understanding, and maybe allowing questions as you go. These have been some of my best experiences, because everyone is engaged and interested when you are talking about their back pocket.

Presenting to an external audience is a different kettle of fish. Hopefully, you will have had a chance to evaluate the nature and make-up of the audience. You now have the tricky job of positioning your talk to not lose too many at the lowest point of understanding, nor lose to boredom those with a good level of understanding. To resolve this, it's often a good idea to tell the audience you will start with a quick summary, and then pick up speed and complexity as you go. Start by reminding the audience of why you're talking to them. You need to establish your credibility so they are prepared to give you a fair chance. Thereafter, start with the basics and then build, with a bigger audience probably asking the chair to hold questions until the end, so that you don't get side-tracked during the available time. Never feel that you have to give them everything. It can be a good idea to leave questions in their mind, so that you get a livelier, but controlled, Q&A.

When you get to the questions at the end of your session, be ready with a pen and paper. Some people ask multiple or lengthy questions, and you need to remind yourself of what they have said before you forget! The advantage of rambling questions is that you can answer as you like, re-emphasising the main points of your presentation. It's not that you're turning into a politician, it's that you want this to be of maximum benefit to everyone there. Sometimes you won't fully understand a question. Say so. And ask them to give you an example, or answer something along the lines of what you think you have heard.

At some conferences you will receive feedback from the organisers. Take it with a pinch of salt and as an opportunity to learn, or, if you're lucky, as an excuse for celebration. If there is a video of the talk, ask for a copy and study it at your leisure, and learn that next time you should keep your hands out of your pockets, or from flicking your hair back all the time. Lots of people practise in front of a mobile phone before giving a big speech, which can be really helpful.

Other tips I have learned the hard way are to have a set of backup notes just in case the projection system fails and you're asked to go ahead anyway without a set of slides (this is why I always ask for a flip chart and pens to be ready at side stage – if not used for the main presentation, I will often use it in the Q&A); wear clothes that give you confidence (my MRC partner, Rebecca Leigh, swore by high heels – she only ever wore them for presentations and weddings); go and rehearse in the room itself, sit at the very back and check your slides are readable, get comfortable with the space; find out where the nearest toilet is; have a bottle of water ready in case they forget to provide one; get to know the chair of the session before the day, or at least before the presentation; have an extra shirt or blouse in a bag (twice I've had problems with soup or spaghetti at the lunch before my session as my nerves kicked in); and always volunteer to go first (you don't want to follow a speaker trained in the dark art of Ted Talks).

If you know that you're really awful when it comes to presenting to groups, then undertake a proper presentation skills training programme. Even if your organisation won't pay (very rare), it's still worth the investment of your time and money. Of all the programmes I have witnessed, the best ones are usually run by people who teach actors to work on stage in front of a live audience. They will spend time with you, getting you to think about poise, clothing, breathing, deportment and voice projection, all key to a killer presentation, as well as the importance of learning by rote the first few lines of your speech, if not all of it.

Try to have fun. By my fifth presentation, I was up and running, and by my tenth, you couldn't stop me. Indeed, if you have to repeat a presentation multiple times to different audiences, it's best to share the load with a colleague. Rebecca and I would switch sections of the speech so that we didn't get complacent, and we would have little competitions about answering each other's questions from the audience.

Probation

What is the point of probation? I ask this at every organisation I join and, in most cases, get it removed. All probation does is make line mangers lazy and sloppy in their recruitment, thinking that they can dispense with someone before the six months is up. I have even known some experienced candidates turn down roles because they don't want to leave their current employer and run the risk of being fired with no compensation six months later. Instead, ensure you have a good recruitment process that hires the person with the right skills and experience for the role, and then make them an offer without probation. If they run into problems, then treat them as you would anyone else, by offering them appropriate help, support and training, and giving them targets to achieve until they reach the required standard.

Productivity

When I'm trying to think through an issue, I am constantly thinking about what will be the best outcome for the business. And in most cases, it's about finding a solution that leads to increased productivity. This is such an important aspect of working life, that I have used it to justify many different projects and change programmes that I have run, sometimes in the face of initial scepticism, or concern about the start-up costs, from colleagues in other teams.

A business will only succeed in the longer term if it has a productive and engaged team of people working in it, that constantly seek small improvements in everything they do, and occasionally step back to review the bigger picture, and undertake a much larger review. If we use gardening as an analogy, to get the best from your crops you need to remove the weeds on a regular basis, but every so often you have to change the rotation to replenish the soil with the right nutrients.

A productivity change at its simplest can be reorganising the flow of work through a department, ensuring that the people with the right skills are employed at each step. It doesn't mean we have to replicate a production line and make people's jobs revolve around a small number of repeated actions, a mistake I have seen many times, especially in finance departments.

As with so many aspects of working with people, the importance of any change is to explain to the whole team what your intentions are, and what you are trying to do. You need to involve them in the change from an early stage, as they will often have ideas and things that they want to input. Indeed, at one company, all I had to do was ask for suggestions to make the data entry jobs more interesting and more productive, and I was snowed under within minutes. As mentioned elsewhere, but worth repeating: an effective technique is to ask people in small groups to describe the most productive arrangements for their work, and what 'perfect' would look like; then ask them to describe the current situation, and work with everyone on how to narrow the gap between the two.

Changes to the structure of a working environment can have cost implications, and this is where sometimes even the best ideas will get parked, but it is always best to work them through as far as you can. Sometimes you will be pleasantly surprised that the director controlling the budget will take the initiative and make the changes. The trick is to look at the costs and time taken (both are entwined) in the current state, and then estimate what the benefits of the changed system will be. If you can generate a return on investment over a year or less, you will have a much better chance of getting the go-ahead. When looking at costs, always factor in the likely impact on turnover. Remember that if you can reduce the possibility of just one person leaving, you can save anywhere between six and twelve months of salary equivalent in hiring and retraining a replacement.

79

Projects

One of the most important tools in the box. Projects give you, personally, an opportunity to shine in cross-functional groups, and the opportunity to share invaluable experience with your team members, and see what they are capable of when either leading or participating. A mix of small and larger projects, with everyone getting involved and reporting back, makes for the best experience.

The role of a project leader should not be underestimated. Training is essential for the uninitiated. Not everyone needs to, or is suitable to be put forward for, PRINCE2 or an equivalent, but everyone needs to get a chance to think about things like the importance of stakeholders in the project, communications, planning, ensuring sufficient resources, and keeping people motivated. These can be learned from far simpler courses, many of which are available online at little or no cost.

Projects should not be the reserve of senior leaders. In my experience some of the best ideas for change and action have come from projects led and run by executive and personal assistants, or by trade union reps, backed by their regional officers.

80

Promotion

When I look at someone's CV, I'm always impressed when they demonstrate an internal promotion. It shows that they have proven themselves, that they have been accepted within the organisation, and that they have the ability to develop and grow.

When leading teams, the promotion of one person sends all sorts of messages, so it needs to be thought-through and, if it's your own team, calibrated with others. Handled badly, the promotion of one person can send a message to another that they will never get promoted, and lead them to move on. Even worse, it can lead to resignation if the promotee is now put in charge of their former colleagues. Often a way around this is to ask the person to lead a project, maybe in another area, and then to come back into a newly promoted role. At other times it just needs to be done, with an honest conversation with any disappointed people about their development needs. To avoid some of these issues it is nearly always best to advertise an opportunity and then interview those interested, alongside a senior manager from another division. Sometimes you will get a pleasant surprise, sometimes you won't, but at least you will have given everyone a fair opportunity. The eventual promotee gets the role in the knowledge that they weren't merely anointed, but instead had to make a case for their promotion, an act that will give them confidence. Always remember that some people will need a push to apply. They may well be fully competent but lack confidence, or assume that the words in the desirable category are essential, and that they don't have all of them.

Every so often you realise that an internal promotion hasn't worked out. The good news is that you gave the benefit of the doubt to an internal candidate, even though it has run into difficulties. Sometimes things can be resolved by internal support, sometimes external coaching might be needed, but every so often the promotion has to be unpicked. The important thing will be maintaining dignity, which a straight move back to the old role would not achieve (aside from the fact that the old job has probably been filled).

What are the alternatives? Asking the person to lead a project, or to review a previous project, or take a secondment to another area (even a supplier), can be an effective way to maintain dignity. You can ask an interim to cover the role whilst you find the right person to take over, or whilst you re-evaluate the role itself. Another route is to restructure, eliminate the role with a flatter structure and then find a suitable alternative role for the failing manager, but without people leadership responsibilities.

81

Racism

It's 2020, so why do I even need a section on racism, FFS? Wealthy black people are documented to have arrived at least as early as the Romans did in the UK, and maybe before. One of Henry VII's paid team of trumpeters was black. People from both African and Asian ethnic descent fought in two world wars, and have played a huge part in the development of civilization. Surely by now we would have stopped making judgements based on skin colour?

To those of you who think that racism doesn't exist, please offer to mentor a range of people with different ethnic backgrounds. You will start asking yourself: why are they stopped and searched regularly, when I am not?; why do they have to apply for twice as many jobs to get an interview, unless they change their name to Smith or Jones?; why do people cross the road (pre-COVID as well) to walk on the other side?; why do they see no role models on interview or speaker panels or in positions of authority in most organisations? I could go on.

The most powerful moment came for me when I watched the videos of the experiments run in the States, and later in the UK, with school kids and adults. Google 'Jane Elliott Iowa'. She is an amazing diversity teacher who segregated students based on eye colour. In just a few hours she had blue-eyed students passionately discriminating against brown-eyed students, and then vice versa. If you haven't seen it, it's scary, but it will make you think long and hard about discrimination. Hopefully, you will then seek ways to reduce and fight back against racism, whether it be overt (rare) or below the surface (surprisingly common).

In the same way that you try to ensure a gender balance when you form project groups, shortlists for a job, or interview panels themselves, think about the ethnic balance as well. Whatever your colour, become an ally or a mentor, and challenge the status quo. This is one area where you can make a difference in HR, whatever level you work at.

82

Recruitment

In the past, recruitment was carried out by HR generalists. A job specification or role description was prepared with the line manager, often a straight update of what had gone before, someone signed off the role, and an advert was prepared, inviting people to send in their CVs or complete an application form. As companies began to recognise just how important it was to find skilled people and hold onto them, people started to specialise in recruitment, learning the tricks of the trade and recognising where to look for the right candidates, and how to create a healthy pipeline for the line managers they supported. This led to the concept of talent acquisition. It is about having an individual, or team, who keeps in close step with the business, ensuring that the brand as an employer is in sync with the brand of the company (either led by marketing, sales, comms or a mix of all three).

As HR or OD professionals one of our responsibilities is to challenge line managers when they come seeking our help to recruit. Are they being lazy when they say they want to replace someone leaving with a carbon copy? Is this an opportunity to develop a more junior member of the team, to divide the role up and recreate new roles instead, to not replace at all and use the money saved in some other way, to promote a current member of the team, to move someone sideways from another part of the organisation, or at the very least to give them a chance to act up whilst you consider them for the bigger role?

Specialists in talent acquisition make it their business to understand the market; to look both long and short term at where the talented recruits will come from; to work alongside universities or colleges, track talented people and keep in touch with them, and set up means to keep in touch with alumni (those who have left, but one day might consider coming back into a bigger role). They can sell the prospect of working for the organisation to anyone they meet online, by phone or in person at a trade or other recruitment event. It's not hard to justify the costs of a talent acquisition specialist, especially if you have been spending a lot on agencies or headhunters, or have a high staff turnover.

Talented people can, of course, be acquired through traditional adverts, via agencies or through search firms. Temps or contractors can help fill a need at speed, and will often make a good impression over time, such that they get recruited into an established vacancy. By tracking talented people, a vacancy can be filled by calling them up and inviting them back for a chat.

All these alternative methods need to be considered in the light of the need to be diverse and inclusive. Sometimes always filling in from within, or only talking to people that have been scouted in the past, denies you the opportunity to test the market and see who is available and potentially increase your diversity as a consequence.

83

Recruitment Agencies

There are multiple agencies and headhunters out there, all keen for your lucrative business. As in so many lines of life, the best ones have the best people working for them. The trick therefore is to find the best consultants in each sector and then follow them when they move between agencies.

'Horses for courses' is a key phrase here. If you want to hire a temporary PA to cover for a holiday, then it's often the case that a local recruitment agency, reliant on a couple of owner consultants who know the area really well, can ensure you get someone that will be reliable and capable. Ideally, you should meet them before the need occurs. When you talk, do they listen and then change their pitch accordingly, or do they stick to the script and keep selling? I know who I would prefer to work with. Some of the major high street agencies can work well, but beware as often they have sales targets to hit and are more bothered by the quarterly bonus (given they are probably leaving after that), than building their reputation over a longer period, which a local owner will want to achieve. One agency that I worked with for many years started off on the right foot by saying that they didn't have anyone with the right skill set and didn't want to risk sending me a less experienced receptionist. After that I felt I could trust them.

Agencies are great for quickly finding temporary and interim staff. And a lot of them specialise in doing just that. When reaching an agreement to work with them, agree up-front what will happen should you wish to offer one of their temps, or interims, an established role. The best agencies have a fee structure for transfer that costs less per month than you employ the person as a temp. Let's say that if you make a permanent offer in the first month, they might expect a fee of 15 to 20% of the annual remuneration, but that should be down to 5 to 10% a few months later. Agencies need to make their margins, so don't expect to get a free transfer.

National agencies can also be helpful in finding specialists on a permanent basis, whether they be in IT or finance, or even in Human Resources. Expect to pay a fee of around 20% of the expected salary plus expenses, but know that much of the hassle of a full recruitment campaign will be removed. Of course, if they want your business in the future, they will put effort into putting forward a good shortlist. It's worth noting that if you state upfront that you want to see a diversity of gender, ethnicity, etc, that most agencies will love the challenge and ensure they meet your brief. They normally only charge their fee once the placement is made, although expenses will be charged regardless.

For more specialist senior roles, and especially exec appointments, the executive search agencies, also known as headhunters, step in to play their part. They will charge around 30% of total remuneration, plus expenses. For the extra cost they will use researchers (sometimes in-house, sometimes freelance), who will search databases such as LinkedIn and their own files, and call up experts in the field, to ask either if they are interested in the role, or if they can recommend others who could be ideal. After a few weeks of calls and initial meetings, the lead consultant will present a longlist of candidates to you and the hiring manager. This is a great opportunity to refine the job search criteria, by rejecting some of their proposed candidates and requesting more information on others. Headhunters usually charge in thirds (up front, on presentation of a shortlist and on placement), and some HR directors will insist on a fixed fee, to avoid the temptation of the headhunter to keep extolling the virtues of yet more expensive candidates. If you pull out of an assignment you will likely pay the majority of their costs, so always check the terms and conditions before signing.

Given that using agencies will cost more money than a simple internet posting or job advert, it's important to agree with the line manager where the budget will come from. It's also important to book diary slots in advance for the longlist, shortlist meetings and for the interviews. This is even more important for senior exec appointments, as getting time in diaries at the last minute can be impossible, and you risk losing the best candidates if you delay the process too long.

Redundancies

At some point in your career you will be involved in making redundancies at your workplace. If you have managed to get close to the business you will know in advance, and can potentially influence the way it works. Sometimes, however, you won't know until the last minute, and this is often the case in large organisations.

The first issue is to try to understand what the proposed redundancies are attempting to achieve. How you handle a need to reduce costs by 10% is different to a decision not to support a project or a product any more. In the former case, you might be able to identify a range of measures short of redundancy that will reduce costs, whilst in the latter, you are closing down a group of people and the alternative to redundancy might be redeployment (maybe with training) to other work groups.

Once you have worked with the line managers to identify exactly which redundancies need to be achieved, you need to develop a draft timeline and communications plan. By developing a timeline between the Human Resources team and the line managers, everyone gets a better understanding of the process and starts to buy into it, as well as realising the time commitments that are necessary for success. The communications plan spells out who is responsible for what, and is clearly linked to the timelines. The comms person can start preparing draft announcements well in advance for all the possible eventualities, saving time when things get tough.

Where there are unions or staff consultative representatives they need to be briefed, possibly in confidence if the change is still not known by the main workforce. By briefing them first you can clear up any early misunderstandings, and start to get an idea of what their objections will be. It also gives you the chance to build relationships with them and hopefully establishes initial trust.

For me this is where the honest, open approach is best. You state what needs to be achieved and why, and then you look for their help in achieving it. If you hide information behind a confidentiality cloak, you will only do yourself a disservice. This is not a power play or a point-scoring opportunity: this is a chance to work together for the good of others.

Some union and staff reps will oppose any redundancies on principle. No union or set of staff reps can be seen to actively support redundancies. You need to talk to them in confidence to explain that you understand their formal response, but given this has to happen, how can you make it easier on the staff they represent?

As a direct consequence of consulting early with staff representatives, I have seen additional ways of saving money identified, I've seen offers to work a reduced week, or stop overtime, to keep people employed, and I've had some excellent debates about how to run a voluntary redundancy (VR) scheme. VR always seems to raise the hackles of line managers, who fear they will lose their best people, but my counter argument is that you will lose those people anyway if you dictate too strongly how and what happens. Way better that you give those people who are ready to make a move a voluntary package and the chance to leave with dignity, than refuse and watch them leave anyway.

In declaring a VR scheme I've always avoided enhanced payments, whilst others insist that there needs to be an incentive. In my view people should make the tough choice without financial inducement, and instead be offered greater flexibility about leaving dates and notice periods. In that way the people who volunteer know they can negotiate their leave date (within a reasonable time frame), that they can leave early with their package if they find an alternative, and that they can choose their own leaving party date should they wish. For those made redundant under compulsory terms after the volunteers have been resolved, the timing usually dictates there is no flexibility left and there is one bigger shared leaving party.

When offering voluntary redundancy, it is important to set a clear time and date by which people make their application, and it's crucial to say upfront which areas you are accepting volunteers from. You should state how long it will take to finalise agreements after the deadline (as short as possible), and have a way to produce redundancy quotes quickly and safely. The reason for this is that you need to give as much certainty as possible. Managing expectations is key, as this is a sensitive issue and people are often putting themselves (and sometimes their partners) under stress by applying, so they need fast responses and appropriate support. Therefore, making sure that all the key line managers reserve a significant chunk of their time on and around deadline day will be key.

In thinking about which staff groups you will allow to apply, you need to be open to the idea of bumping, and make provision for it. Simply put, this is where you allow a voluntary redundancy from an unaffected area to create an opportunity for someone under threat of redundancy to transfer to. Let's say we need to reduce our procurement team by three, but only two are volunteering. By accepting volunteers from finance, we can create a vacancy for the last procurement person to redeploy into. In my experience, those people are so pleased to be staying that they work flat out for it to be a success. A terrific example I had was when two IT help desk workers came to me and volunteered to halve their hours and work as a job share, to save anyone else in their team being made redundant. It worked really well.

Bumping is closely linked to the issue of pools. When making a selection for redundancy, or setting the boundaries from where you will accept volunteers, you will often (and especially in larger organisations), define the types of employees that you will be selecting from. These form the pools from which you then make redundancies. And they can be quite tricky to get right. An example is a sales team. In the group you will probably have sales people with different levels of experience, analysts, administrators, and maybe business development staff. If you need to reduce the number of sales reps by territory, the pool might well be easy to define by a geographic boundary, but would you accept volunteers from a neighbouring team? If you need to reduce admin support, do you select the pool from within the sales division, or do you open it out across the whole company?

Having defined your pools and set out your rationale for VR and run your process, do you know how you will resolve the issue of all four specialists volunteering, when you only need to reduce the number by one? These issues point powerfully to the need to consult and get agreement before proceeding.

Once you have worked through the issues and formally accept a volunteer for redundancy, you will need to agree the dates and the overall package (hopefully this will include Outplacement), it is a good idea to have a signed agreement (maybe a legally binding Settlement Agreement), and this is where you will maybe want an employment lawyer to confirm you have got everything right. I say maybe, because it is not always necessary. If you have had good support from the unions or the staff reps, then a signed letter from the employee to the company confirming they are volunteering for redundancy, with the main details covered, is often all that is needed.

On many occasions I have had people ask me after the deadline if they can now be given VR. Call me cynical, but in most cases I suspect this happens because they have found another job elsewhere and would love to exit with some redundancy pay. But there are genuine cases where someone is inspired by the acts of others, wants to be selfless and is genuinely wanting to protect others by volunteering. In such cases I've tried to be as flexible as possible, because making a compulsory redundancy is so much harder on the people concerned, especially if they know that volunteers have been turned down.

Moving on, your volunteers have all been accounted for and you still have to reduce the people left behind. You need to get all the key managers in a room, possibly off-site, work though the organisation design and then go through the arduous task of selecting who should go. People will say that you should use performance records, appraisals, sickness absence data, length of service, etc, and yes, everything needs to be considered, but whatever factors you use, the key is to have a consistent logic and to ensure that fairness comes into play. If one of the people made redundant attended a tribunal, would you have a reasonable case to have made them redundant? This is why, of course, many organisations still revert to first in, last out. In other words, you make the process of selection easy by giving preference to your longest-serving members of staff. The comfort of this approach is that you have a system that is easy to understand and hard to fight, but may well remove some of the best talent that you have recruited in recent years in one fell swoop.

Once you have made your selections, you need to coach your line managers in how to tell their staff. In my view it's usually best for the line manager and a member of Human Resources to meet them in a private space, with at least half-hour intervals. Remember that once the line manager has said to the person that they are being made redundant, you will encounter a range of reactions, and you should never try to second-guess who will react in what way. It is worth remembering that many people go into shock, and can't hear anything that is said after the word 'redundancy'. Having a straightforward confirmatory letter for them to take away with them, which includes a paragraph on where to turn if they need support, is important here. That shock might account for a lack of any questions, which is why you need to make time available later that day, or the next day, to talk this through with them, when all the questions have developed. Anger does occur, and sometimes the first response is shouting about being picked on or how unfair it is. Absolute silence accompanied by a hard stare still makes me shiver. Even tougher is when the person says something like 'I didn't volunteer because my partner has just been diagnosed with cancer and I need stable employment.'

On the bright side, I still clearly remember a young lab technician, whom I had been dreading telling, leap up in excitement when I told him he was being made redundant and give me a hug. He explained that he had wanted to volunteer, but his girlfriend hadn't let him. He was now going to use the money to tour with his band! I'm not sure his relationship survived, but his band did quite well.

Once everyone has been told (including those away from work) and they have received their initial letters, you need to announce to everyone that the process has now been completed, otherwise they will continue to be on edge and under stress. People need to talk these things through so, whatever you do, don't tell everyone to get back to work straightaway. Accept that there will be a lack of productivity as things settle down.

Find some time to talk through what has happened with the line managers that have had to tell their staff they are redundant. A chance to talk is key to helping them come to terms with the redundancies, and will help you build stronger relationships for the future. Be ready to just listen, whether over a tea/coffee or something stronger. The same applies to your Human Resources colleagues, especially those for whom redundancies are a new experience. And don't forget the admin team. Often having to prepare all those letters, agreements and payroll changes can be distressing, especially as the chances are they will be making some of their friends redundant.

Be ready in the coming weeks to show flexibility and allow people to leave early, maybe reverse a decision on appeal if the reasons are sound, and remember to support those who are staying: they might be suffering from survivor syndrome and need encouragement to rebuild their teams and ensure the future is strong. Some will be suffering from imposter syndrome and feel they are not as worthy as other colleagues made redundant. Your job is to ensure that they quickly regain their confidence and become productive again.

During this phase it's a good idea to monitor social media, or at least alert your comms team to do so. In particular, you need to look at specialist sites like Glassdoor, and be ready to answer complaints that are raised. Ignoring them looks bad; dealing with them empathetically, yet firmly, will send good signals to future potential applicants reviewing the site.

After a round of redundancies, the one thing that you want to ensure is that the people who are remaining feel as secure as possible. If a senior manager is concerned they haven't made sufficient cuts, help them to understand that a second round of redundancies will only lead to widespread insecurity and resignations. Much better to simply not replace any future leavers (there will be some, because your actions will have already unsettled people) and find cost reductions in other ways if possible. Communications can help at this stage, such as a note confirming the impact of the redundancies is that sufficient costs have been saved, as can positive projects for change and rebuilding.

Some companies are embarrassed about redundancies and want to sweep them under the carpet as quickly as they can. This can be a mistake. Each redundant person has colleagues or friends, sometimes relatives at work, so they need to be treated with help, support, respect and dignity. That should include a proper leaving do, where they want it, as well as the usual cards and presents and speeches if that is the tradition.

Once everything has been completed it can be useful, and cathartic, to write a short report for your management or exec group that covers the key events, the learnings and what to do more or less of, if ever the process has to be repeated.

If you are personally affected by the redundancy then also read the chapter entitled (Being Made) Redundant, which is aimed at Human Resources people.

85

(Being Made) Redundant

Redundancy is a fact of life, and the most difficult thing as a Human Resources person is when you are faced with it yourself, you don't always have an HR person to turn to, and yet others still need your support. Simultaneously, you have to work hard to get through the initial anger (unless you volunteered) to remain professional and stay focused on moving forwards after you have left.

If you are offered Outplacement (see the corresponding chapter), then take it. If it's not offered, ask for it. Don't assume that because you work in HR that you can do everything for yourself (remember the story of the cobbler's children who have no shoes?). Argue that others have you to support them, but you need your own support. Even though you are trained in this field, you will still benefit from the perspective of a neutral third party. Don't wait until you have left; meet your consultant early. Talk through your concerns, let out any anger, and build a plan that you can focus on.

For me, outplacement provided a wake-up call. My personal job search technique was rusty, my CV was full of older jobs and I was missing an edge. My outplacement consultant helped me through this maze, rehearsed my interview technique as a candidate and, as a consequence, finding a new role became a lot easier. Most importantly though, I learned that I needed to put aside some quality time each day to concentrate on myself, and how I would move forward.

Hopefully, you will have one or more mentors. Involve them early, and work with them to keep things in perspective. Use the redundancy to reassess where you are in your career. Do you want more of the same, or is this the moment to try something different? Talking these things through with an outplacement counsellor, a friend or mentor will help. Given the predictions that we will all need to work until we are seventy in the future, do think about taking a proper break from everything, assuming you receive a redundancy payment. As you can normally avoid paying income tax on the first £30k of a redundancy payment in the UK, you can divide the sum you will receive by your current net monthly pay, to work out how many months you will be covered. This helps with perspective and liberates you to think about taking off a month or more to travel the world, or whatever takes your fancy.

I've found that in speaking to headhunters and during interviews, it's best to be honest and explain that there was a restructuring, that you are now redundant and looking for your next opportunity. Never rubbish the old employer, it just doesn't work! Try not to accept the first thing that comes along, or if you are tempted, make sure you seek the advice of someone you trust first, just to check your motivation. I've known people take something just to get one back on their old line manager, only to realise later that they compounded a bad situation.

References

Offers of employment are often made subject to references, and sometimes to medicals. Increasingly references are bland, and merely confirm the dates the person worked for the employer and their role title. I guess they help identify anyone who has completely made up a story about being employed, but that is all they do. Some recruitment consultants pride themselves on their ability to source a more detailed character reference, and by checking qualifications back to source. They do this by directly calling a line manager known to them and asking for details, often using a prepared set of questions to guide them. These can be useful, but even then, they have to be taken with a pinch of salt. It is, after all, in their interests that the person is confirmed in the role before they get their final fee.

When asked for a reference, I have always tried to respond as quickly as I can, knowing that someone's next move might be held up if I don't. I believe I have to be honest. My own reputation is on the line. This has led to me giving basic, minimal responses on several occasions, when I wouldn't have wanted that person back in my team, for example. Remember that in many countries, references are 'discoverable', meaning that the person you are providing a reference for may well see it at some point in the future.

Relative Deprivation

When studying for my CIPD exams I learned an awful lot of theories, read some dreadful 'essential' books, learned all about laws and more importantly case law, and swatted up on many out-of-date practices to get my qualification. Yet for some unknown reason, I was never taught about Relative Deprivation or Discretionary Effort. No one recommended that I read *Maverick!* by Ricardo Semler or *The Prince* by Niccolo Machiavelli. Why? Well, I guess the cynical answer is that they weren't written by CIPD examiners and so had no place on the curriculum. But neither was the Equalities Act, so that rules out that idea.

Maybe 'they' want a conservative set of Human Resources professionals who are all compliant and spend their time trying to interpret the staff handbook, rather than rewrite or destroy it, and the rest of their time trying to either increase meaningless scores in staff attitude surveys or hire sufficient people to replace all those that have left since the last payroll was run. But back to the chapter...

Relative Deprivation is best exemplified by the hiring process. An advert goes up and states £28k basic pay. Fred is currently on £25k at a competitor (like all his colleagues), and applies for the role. He gets the job and is very happy. Relative to all the colleagues he left behind, he is now £250 a month better off.

Two weeks later, Fred chats to Freda. She's doing exactly the same job, same hours, same building at his new company. Freda has been there a month longer, was earning £27k and is now earning £29k. Relative to Freda, Fred is now underpaid, and he feels relatively deprived.

In the space of two weeks he has gone from being very happy to being annoyed. Indeed, he is already actively thinking about ways to work to rule, i.e. to not give any extra. His discretionary effort just went down the pan.

We all have a job to do and normally some sort of role description. The Discretionary Effort that we give is the extra that we put in place above and beyond the minimum expected of us. When we are enjoying our work, respect our line managers and like our company, we are more likely to give a bit extra, work a bit harder, and go a bit beyond our role. That is the extra discretionary effort that we give, often with no payback other than the satisfaction of a job well done.

Semler, in his series of books and articles written in the 1990s after he had taken over the family business in Brazil, gives us a fascinating insight into a world where people on the shop floor dramatically increased their productivity once they were involved in the running of the organisation. They were encouraged to give additional discretionary effort by Semler and his managers, incidentally managers who were often appointed by the workers themselves.

Semler goes on to break several taboo subjects, such as the idea of publishing all salaries and getting a debate going about what a role is worth in cash terms, for example, the difference between experience gained on the shop floor, compared to new insights from outside. Even now when you read his work, you are wondering if this is even possible, and the reality is that it is now twenty-five years since he was practising it.

And Machiavelli? We often state that people are being Machiavellian when we believe they are twisting or manipulating things. But a read of *The Prince* shows that he was simply an incredible observer of human beings and of history, and that he used those observations to considerable effect. I will take it as an honour next time I am called Machiavellian.

88

Relocation

Whether it's moving a single new recruit, or a whole site, from one place to another, we have to remember that relocation is a big deal, and one of the most stressful things that people have to do in their lives. For recent single graduates straight out of college, and in rental digs, it may be relatively straightforward, but as soon as partners, children, dependent elderly parents and houses to sell and buy are factored in, then you can't be sure that the relocation will proceed to conclusion.

Treat each relocation as a separate event, made different by the fact that everyone presents with different circumstances. If you have the budget, think about using specialist relocation services: people who can advise on schools, take people on familiarisation tours, arrange bridging finance and mortgages, help find jobs for partners, source quotes for removals and change utility suppliers, find temporary accommodation as needed, amongst many other things. If your budget is limited, then you will need to provide extra paid time off for people to undertake their own searches and move. And whatever your budget, you will need to reimburse some of the costs of moving, even if you apply a cap, otherwise you are either damning your people to an unproductive lengthy commute, or risking losing them to other employers.

Large-scale relocations of offices or factories need careful planning. Unless you have someone in your team that is an exceptional project manager, now is the time to hire a contractor. And that is just for the employee relations – I'm assuming that the facilities team will take responsibility for the physical relocation of the contents. When moving several major facilities and staff from Greenford, Ware and Beckenham to Stevenage, we set up a small dedicated relocation team and helped employees and their families get excited about the move by taking them on regular coach trips to see the new building as it emerged from the ground, as well as trips to view housing in nearby areas, visits to schools and colleges. We also provided support to partners who would need to seek new opportunities. An operation like this isn't cheap, until you recognise the retention of so many important staff and the reduced costs of having to recruit and train new team members.

89

Remuneration Committee

If you are in a small company then you might get the opportunity to attend a Remuneration Committee (RemCo) sooner in your career than in a larger organisation, but from an early stage be on the lookout for opportunities to volunteer to get involved, such as suggesting that you present some data to them around the outcome of the pay review, or performance measures you are proud of. An easy entry route is to volunteer and sit silently, taking minutes of the meetings. Just being there and listening to the debate will give you great experience.

RemCo is usually made up of a small number of non-exec directors who represent the shareholders or trustees, and have the task of ensuring that the Chief Executive is held to account when making decisions about pay, bonus and benefits, as well as setting the terms for the CEO and other exec members. The CEO attends and in addition there is usually a secretary to the committee. RemCo has the power to appoint advisors, and often these are reward specialists who work for consulting firms with access to average pay and bonus and share option data for similar-sized organisations.

Given that their role is to oversee the work and pay of the executive team, your role is to ensure they have everything they need to achieve that goal. If, for example, there is a proposal by the CEO to hire a new CFO (Chief Finance Officer), your role is to research the pay rates for CFOs in similar organisations and make notes about the pay and benefits the previous CFO received. You'll need to do the same for other benefits and then separately prepare tables of share options granted historically (if your organisation offers them) and any conditions that should be applied. Even if you don't currently have a CFO, your financial controller should be able to help, or get support from a legal team or a specialist reward consultancy.

If you are the Secretary for the meeting, then well ahead of the meeting have a chat with your CEO about what they want to achieve, prepare an agenda and then have a chat with the Chair and get their agreement. Make sure that the last set of minutes goes out with the agenda to the members and any papers that you want them to read in advance. Be ready on the day to have to set up a teleconference at the last minute: it has happened to me so many times I just assume it these days! One of the best RemCo Chairs I have worked with is Sir Donald Brydon CBE, distinguished in my mind for always finding the time to chat through an agenda in advance of a meeting, his excellent skills in chairing each item to a successful conclusion, his desire for fairness and integrity, and his resolve to see actions undertaken subsequently.

When preparing papers, try to put yourself in the shoes of the directors, remember that they don't work at the organisation and so might need additional background information. Try to second-guess any questions they may have. And the good news is, in all my time on committees I have never known anyone try to catch me out; all I have encountered is genuine questions and lots of support and sometimes some great advice.

90

Resigning

Assuming you are determined to leave and don't want to use the external offer as a lever for renegotiating your current contract, then the best advice is to wait until you have an unconditional offer. If the new company says they are offering the job pending references and a medical, then you need to clear both to be safe.

Having said that, many people resign much earlier. Sometimes there is a high degree of trust and confidence in the conditions being met, so waiting is deemed unnecessary, and I've known one person who was so keen to leave that they weren't that bothered if the new job didn't work out, they just needed an excuse to escape. The most common reason is that to get the reference the new employer is going to need, then why not package the explanation about leaving with the reference request at the same time?

When you do resign, remember that a gap in employment could mean you have no life or health insurance, so sometimes it's best to keep a small gap, or take holiday from your old employer to cover the gap.

The best way to resign is to chat to your line manager first. Ask for a private meeting, in an office, or in a busy café. You want to ensure it is just the two of you. Have your written letter ready, concealed in a folder. Avoid work conversation, and simply say, 'I've asked for a private meeting, because I wanted you to be the first to know that I am resigning. I'm on [X] months' notice, but I would be very grateful if you would release me on [date], so that I can start my new role on the following Monday.' By doing this you are signalling that the only negotiation is on the date.

When asked why, simplicity is key: 'I've been thinking about my career next steps, and the opportunity I've been given looks superb.'

In conversation, tell them that you have really enjoyed working with them and for the organisation, but that the time has come for a new challenge. Allow for a discussion and maybe a pitch by your manager to try to persuade you to stay.

Once completed, hand over your signed letter, formally confirming your resignation and dates that you hope to work to. Many times, a request to leave before your notice period ends will be accepted because they know that your mind will be elsewhere, albeit it may take a day or so for them to get their head around it. Be ready to work your full notice, especially if your division is in a heavy period of workload, you are involved in a key project, or you have specialist knowledge that needs to be transferred to others.

You don't have to say where you are going but, if it is to a competitor, then you may be asked to go on gardening leave, especially if they are concerned about trade secrets or access to confidential or sensitive data. In such a circumstance you are entitled to all your pay and benefits during the period. Take it with grace and enjoy the break (you'll need it). Keep things as civil as you can, especially if you need a reference, and move on to how to pass your work over to others before you leave. If you have people working for you, let them know personally as soon as you can, remembering that the rumour mill will travel at electronic speed.

Returning to work

If you have been away for a while, or you are the HR person responsible for someone returning, then advance preparation is key.

In the case of sickness, you will need a doctor's note confirming fitness for work and what, if any, support or restrictions are needed. Someone returning after major surgery might require support getting to and from work, workplace adjustments (table, chair, laptop), reduced hours (e.g. avoiding rush hour), or even an evacuation plan with the fire marshals, if not fully ambulant.

The line manager needs to be fully on-board and ready to put out the welcome mat. Hopefully, they have been involved in a series of keeping in touch days, or regular calls/emails depending upon the circumstances. Good practice is for the line manager to meet the returnee a week or so before they start at a neutral venue, such as a coffee shop near where the returnee lives.

On the day itself, maybe ask someone to meet the returnee outside and walk in with them. That way they can clear security easily if their pass doesn't work, and it will take the strain off having to stop and chat to everyone on the way to the desk.

Day One is not the day for the person to try and catch up on everything. Just sorting out IT systems and sharing news about the return will be tiring on its own. One tip is to suggest a coffee mid-morning with cakes; that way the news can be shared once with everyone, rather than repeated *ad nauseum*.

Reward

When you work in a small HR team, you probably won't have the luxury of a specialist reward person, unless you have complex bonus or share option arrangements (although, where possible, allow these to be run by the finance team, who are experts at these types of systems and processes). Selecting a specialist consultant or agency on an as-needed basis will, therefore, be important, as this is an area where you will need access to relevant sector data and the best current thinking about how to reward your employees, or how to resolve questions or disputes about pay when they arise. This will probably be a separate arrangement to that which the Remuneration Committee of the board appoint, to advise them on executive pay, but sometimes it will be the same.

In larger organisations you will either already have a specialist in reward, or you will need to find one, and that is where the fun begins. Good reward people are few and far between. They have the ability to analyse data, make meaningful and helpful suggestions, influence decision makers and speak plain English. Before going outside to recruit, see if there is someone in your current team who excels with spreadsheets and enjoys analysing data. Ask them to try out the role, maybe part-time to start with, offering them the opportunity to study further at the organisation's expense (in the UK, the CIPD Level 7 is the award to aim for), and find them a good external mentor or coach. Often this will be far easier than trying to find a recruit, albeit there will always be somebody out there, provided your pay scales are flexible enough to accommodate them!

Once you have the right expertise and people in place, a review of your total reward and how it compares within your sector is a strong starting point and should precede the proposal of any significant changes to your pay systems. With the continuously changing face of reward, this is pretty much essential every ten years, and preferably every five years, with annual or biannual checks. Some sectors move so fast that reward reviews have to be undertaken at least every year. The IT division will often tell you they have the greatest need for regular review, but look also at the departments where the wealth is generated for your organisation. Get their pay wrong and you will not be thanked by the exec team.

In making fundamental changes to reward systems (as opposed to the annual review and a small percentage increase for all), it is important to model the impact on all the people in the organisation. Such modelling takes time, but is key to being able to predict those groups who may feel relatively deprived compared with others, or those where there will be a significant impact, e.g. where you may have to red ring (or red circle) pay for a period. Red ringing is not a scientific method, it is simply the act of freezing someone's pay, whilst the market rates (internally and/or externally) catch up. On the occasion that you find some people are underpaid against the market, you may also find that your organisation doesn't have the ability to pay at the appropriate level straight away. In such cases it is important to be honest and open with the affected employees, and let them know how you will redress the balance over time. If the pay issue is gender specific, you may have no option but to move to make the change quickly.

When reviewing reward systems, or discussing them with current or prospective employees, remember that total reward is just as important as base pay. This is particularly true with local government and other public service roles, where the base pay may be low when compared with others in the area, but is more than made up for by the increased benefits and provisions, including enhanced pensions, holidays and the like. The difficulty with trying to sell these add-on benefits to prospective employees is that they do not help pay the rent, or create their desired mortgage opportunity. Hence the increasing use of cafeteria benefits, where employees can forego elements of the package that are not attractive to them at that point in their life (e.g. a single person may forego life insurance, whereas a parent with young children may consider that essential).

93

Romantic Liaisons

Whoever you ask about romantic liaisons at work will offer different advice. I've heard some strong lines in the past, such as 'Never date someone at work' through to 'Sure, shall I have a look at his file for you?'. The circumstances do play a part. In a large organisation where you're in different divisions, it can be similar to working in different companies. Whereas, in a small office of ten people, or in the same department of a big division, it can be quite awkward. So, part of the answer will also depend on how maturely the relationship develops, assuming it gets off the ground at all!

The type of business might also have an impact, and indeed its policies. In some high-security places relationships are banned (although that is difficult to police), for fear of compromise or accidental bedside whispers.

My view is simple: it's hard enough to find someone you want to date in this world, let alone someone whom you want to become your partner. Life is too short, so go for it!

If the relationship develops, and there is a potential conflict of interest (especially if you're also the HR person for that area), then tell your line manager straight away. It only makes things worse if you delay. People who try to hide office relationships invariably fail, hence the advice to get it out in the open early. In that way you can be yourself and avoid awkward moments.

Sabbaticals

If you have worked in the same role for a long time you may start to get a bit rusty, or lose motivation in your work. Being honest with your line manager and talking to them about this usually pays dividends. It might be that you can negotiate changes to your role, take on an interesting project, or switch roles between divisions, but there are times when a complete break is needed.

When planned and organised well, a sabbatical can give you the chance to step away from your job for six or twelve months and do something different. Travel the world, write a book, take a diploma at college, work in a charity, train as a coach – the possibilities are endless. By discussing such options early with your line manager, you're giving them a chance to make plans, possibly to recruit an interim, maybe to train or temporarily promote someone, or to tell you about a promotion that is just around the corner for you.

Given how quickly the world moves, and how organisations have to constantly change and adapt to thrive, you have to accept that your old role may not be there for you when you return. This is a risk that you need to accept, but one that usually works out in the end. With your newfound enthusiasm for work and the new skills you will have developed, you will either take back your old role and find it fun again, or be offered another opportunity, maybe leading a project whilst you re-engage.

Sand-pitting

Sand-pitting has been developed from the idea of a child wanting to go and play in another child's sandpit, and discovering new things. In the world of work, it can have a huge impact on productivity, and is a relatively easy project to run, has positive results and makes Human Resources look good for having introduced it. So, what is it?

At a basic level, sand-pitting is a chance for someone from one department to take a week of work experience in another. For example, the chemist in a biotech goes and works with the biologists for a week. To be successful they need to treat it as if they are on holiday from their day job, leaving their normal work behind, and concentrating fully on the new role, working alongside the new team, going to coffee and lunch with them, working their hours, etc.

There's a need for some guidelines, of course. These include: the right to ask questions to understand the new area, as a work experience person would need to do; to get on and be productive in the new role and not challenge everything; to be positive and reflect on good things; and to let people back in their own department know what they learned on return.

At Vernalis, some significant cost savings resulted from one of the chemists telling the biologists that an expensive assay that they ran, as standard, was no longer needed (it had been run for years after a one-off request). At another institute, an accountant was able to dramatically simplify the project worksheets for the researchers after seeing the amount of time they took to complete them, and monthly reports were made biannually instead.

The best way to start out on a sand-pitting project is to find a couple of forward-thinking line managers willing to allow a trial experiment, give it a go, iron out any issues, and then consider inviting more departments to offer experiences, maybe even setting up a scheme to coordinate requests. At Vernalis, we devoted a whole week to people all moving around the building, but this isn't always going to be practical. You also have to take into account busy periods, so the finance team won't be interested at year-end, but might well be a few weeks later.

Some people will object, or express concern about work being interrupted. Any change like this will cause concern, and some will want to avoid being exposed, which is why one of the guidelines is that positive feedback is encouraged. This helps build confidence and goodwill amongst teams, and helps when you want to start the next set moving.

96

Secondments

There are numerous opportunities to use secondments, both within a larger organisation and sometimes outside the company in a smaller one. The legal profession has used them for many years, ensuring that their trainees get experience of working in different specialist areas and on both sides of the client fence. They can be particularly useful within an organisation to cover long-term illness or maternity leave, having the additional benefit of providing invaluable experience to the secondee. They can also work well in a situation where a loyal employee has been in a role a while and needs to be reinvigorated. For HR administrators, a short secondment to the payroll team can be eye-opening, as can an external secondment to the pensions or other benefits administrators.

To ensure success, secondments need to be facilitated by the HR team, acting as a broker to ensure that suitable arrangements are made covering the length of the secondment; what roles the hosting line manager and seconding line manager will play in things like performance management; whether extra pay or bonuses will apply; how the return to the original role will happen; what cover will be provided, if any, in the backfill operation; and sometimes a debate about whether or not it is possible to hold down both jobs at once. Once all is decided an agreement, approved by all three parties, is a good idea, and should include the way in which an early stop should be enacted just as much as an extension.

Some of the most successful secondments I have seen haven't just been about filling a vacancy for a few months; they have been project related with clear boundaries and a measure of success that could be celebrated at the end and added to a CV.

Some organisations ensure fairness in the workplace by advertising secondment opportunities with interviews and proper selection decisions. This can work well, but needs to be treated like an internal vacancy with rigour around role descriptions, selection criteria and equal opportunity to apply.

Most objections to secondments come from the donor line managers, who can be blinkered, only seeing the hassle to them personally rather than the benefit to the employee or the organisation. They will say they are sorry, but the person is involved in a key project that needs to be completed otherwise they will miss their targets, or that their team is settled at the moment and they can't see how the workload will be absorbed. But the key thing is that, without a new challenge of this kind, the employee is likely to be applying for other jobs and moving on soon anyway.

97

Settlement Agreements

Known by the press as gagging orders, settlement agreements (sometimes called by their old name, compromise agreements) are a sensible way to terminate executive employment, or other employment contracts, where trust has broken down and a normal system around grievance or discipline has come unstuck. A good agreement will prevent a lengthy and expensive period of litigation and leave both sides feeling they have won. The essence of an agreement is that the employer makes an additional payment to the employee, normally above that which they would receive if made redundant, in return for a promise that they will not go to a tribunal or any other court after they have left, nor will they publicise the reason for their departure, nor the amount of compensation they have received. The agreement has to be signed by an independent solicitor and paid for by the employer, who takes the employee through all the options and ensures that the agreement is fair.

The best way to achieve a fair agreement is to have a protected conversation with the employee, talking through their options and making an initial offer of the sums you are prepared to pay. If you write these down, always caveat them with the phrase 'subject to contract', which essentially means that nothing is agreed until both sides have signed the contract.

Once the basics around leaving date, compensation and benefits are resolved, a good SA will then include things like an agreed written reference, and will sometimes include the mobile phone and/or laptop (which will need to be wiped by the IT team before it is released). Let the person leave with as much dignity as possible, so an agreed internal communication and a leaving party are also well worth the extra few minutes and pounds.

There are occasions when an employee either doesn't think that the maximum settlement you are offering covers their perceived injustice, or they want their day in court. These can, unfortunately, be spurred on by unscrupulous No Win No Fee agencies, who don't really care what they win. They just want to maximise their revenue steam, and will often settle at the last minute, to the detriment of the ex-employee, once all their fees are removed.

Share Options

A great way to get your employees engaged with the overall success of the business is to be able to offer share options to all. This is particularly true with smaller companies, especially where the pay and bonuses are tight because cash is king. The thought that your hard work and endeavour can result in a pay-out when either the company floats on the stock market, or the options in a traded company mature, can be useful when motivating people. The flip side is also true. When the company is going through a rough patch, or the stock market is undergoing a 'correction', it can be demotivating, and I have been in many more situations where my options have been worthless, compared with the two occasions where they have produced a small bonus.

The levels and numbers of share options, their longevity, the number of times they are issued, and the conditions that apply to them, will all give you fun and games when trying to explain them to employees, and when trying to ensure some kind of equitable arrangement. This is especially so when employees can see just how many options the executives in their company hold, simply by downloading the annual remuneration report. But, for all their problems and administration and payroll and tax implications, they probably have a positive impact on both motivation and retention. Expect the finance team, or the company secretary, to administer them (or to hire an external agency to run the scheme), but you and the HR team will have to get to know the details, because you will be asked plenty of questions about them.

Sleep

Recently I've spent quite a bit of time with senior HR people, and it's interesting that all have suffered a lack of sleep related to work at some point, and all have experienced at least one panic attack, or similar. All said that the intensity of work had increased in the past ten years, driven mostly by mobile comms systems featuring not just text, email and social media, but also a range of project apps and workgroups, which all add to their workload.

There is no universal solution, but the best ones I've tried so far include:

- Not looking at work for at least two hours before you sleep.
- Setting the expectation with colleagues that work hours end at [X] o'clock.
- Have a pad of paper and a pen by your bed, and write down your thoughts and ideas, leaving them for the next day (this somehow clears the brain).
- Avoid obvious things like cheese and caffeine in the evening.
- Undertake some mindfulness exercises.
- Try some cognitive behavioural techniques (searchable on the internet).
- Get some exercise in the evening after you have finished work.
- Talk to HR peers in confidence; share your issues.
- Delegate whole tasks, not bits, and trust your team to deliver.

- At times of peak workload, let colleagues know when you have a full plate, explain that you will get back to them in five days (remember the plumber does this, only handling emergencies in the meantime). To remain credible you need to tell them when you have things back under control.

100

Suicide

It's stomach churning when you hear a colleague has committed suicide (or, more commonly, that they have been found dead and investigations are continuing). Each time I have been left thinking, 'Was there more I could have done?'

After the initial shock, and need to just down tools and chat, you realise that most of your colleagues are thinking the same thing, especially the line manager and immediate peers. And, of course, it is way too easy to blame yourself, especially if you are the line manager, because you could always have done more: you could have stuck with them wherever they went ,for example, but that is never going to be realistic or even desired by the team.

I've lost a member of my family, two members of my rugby club, two friends and four work colleagues, all male, to the same fate. And all bar one of those people was considered the life and soul of the party, which makes it even more strange. Or should I say even more understandable?

In the immediate aftermath of a colleague's suicide you need to alert all key managers and comms teams and then word a sensitive communication to all staff from your CEO, explaining the basics of what is known, reminding people where the colleague worked and on what projects they were focused. Sometimes the wording needs to be agreed with the family, or with the police if they still have an open mind about the reason for the death.

For the team the person worked with a meeting is essential: a chance to stop work, reflect, talk about the person and allow feelings to be expressed. If you don't have an occupational health specialist, it's probably a good idea to invite some counsellors into the offices later that day, the next day and on/off for a couple of weeks. 'Bereavement counsellors' is what you're looking for when searching online, this is their specialism. Don't limit them to the colleague's team, as you won't necessarily know where their friends in the organisation were based. Remember also that this will trigger emotions in those that have already suffered a similar event at some other point in their life.

What can *we* as Human Resources, do going forward to reduce the likelihood of suicide, given that you can't remove it completely? Firstly, we need to ask how people in our teams are. If they say 'fine', we need to ask them again and give them a chance to talk, as many hide their true feelings and need a prompt to open up. Stiff Upper Lips have a lot to answer for.

You can do more. As in *you*! For example, you can set up a network of Mental Health First Aiders. Not only will more people be trained in understanding these issues, but someone might actually be helped in such a way that they don't take their life, or at a simpler level, they might feel better about something they were otherwise worried about.

Additionally, you can talk about your own experiences and help reduce the stigma of talking about mental health issues. You can monitor mental health as a cause of absence, and see how in the past it was probably recorded as stomach aches or similar. And you can check in regularly with your friends and family.

If you're interested in finding out more about Mental Health First Aiders, then Mental Health England is a great place to start (https://mhfaengland.org/), plus they have links to other organisations around the world. Mental Health is covered further in this book.

101

Supporting HR Teams

A good Head of HR will regularly chat to all their team members as a group and as individuals, and will therefore be aware when stress levels are rising and be able to change things around, like priorities, reducing the heat as needed.

Where this is not possible – key times are often during restructuring, merger or TUPE events – then the people to turn to for support include those who are good at helping others regain perspective, reset priorities and see the wood for the trees. They may include:

- Other HR people in the network. Other HR people know the issues, will have personal experience of going through them, will keep matters confidential, and consequently should always be the first point of call. If ever you needed a good reason to grow your network, this is it.
- Occupational Health teams mostly exist in the bigger companies, and hopefully are closely linked to the HR team. They know the company and its staff well and can advise on appropriate courses of action. In smaller companies you might have access to an ERP advisory phone line. Don't assume it is just for staff. Use it for HR issues as well.
- Consultants often hold their roles because they have specialist experience developed over many years in their field. In a case where there is additional workload, or stress in the HR team,

then it might be sensible to consult with someone who has been there before and can help work out where the priorities should be and what could be dropped. You could also ask for practical help in running a project or two, to reduce the load.

- Contractors tend to look for longer projects than consultants, and can be just the right people to turn to when the pressure is on. I have used them often as project managers for big events, like a TUPE, or the implementation of a new system or change in process.
- Mentors can play a big part in helping individuals in the team through the worst, and even though it might seem counterintuitive to be setting this up at a time of high workload, why not? If it helps with perspective and ability to work productively, then it can only be beneficial to all.
- Coaches tend to support the change in behaviour of managers aspiring to be leaders, but they are also key to developing talented people and in helping prioritise, so if you have worked with coaches before, then get back in touch with them for help and support now.

There will also be like-minded or supportive people in the organisation, e.g. MHFAs, comms team, finance people, and working with them on issues keeps things in-house, shares the load and can lead to deeper and more sustained relationships in the future.

102

Surgeries

When you're working in HR, it's not always easy to understand the pressures and challenges facing people in different departments, or the differences in culture and work between them.

For me the best way to find out has always been to take my laptop and go and sit with the group, listening, chatting, going to tea and lunch, where possible for several days at a time so that I become a part of the team. I work on my own things, disappear to make the odd call, leave for a meeting, but just by being present I am able to absorb the atmosphere, understand some of the issues and see how the supervisors and managers interact with their team.

On occasion I will run a timed surgery in their meeting room. These are for thirty-minute booked slots, so that people can come and have a confidential chat about anything they want. For some reason, people are happy to come to an open surgery and talk about their career, a project they are doing, a potential grievance they might have, an issue with a benefit or whatever, that they wouldn't want to trouble me with in my HR office. Surgeries help break down barriers and give additional insights. Outside the office environment, surgeries work well with facilities teams and others, like maintenance engineers, who have a roving or peripatetic role.

An even more immersive experience, and one that has given me some of the best working days of my life, is to take on someone else's role for a week. This involves some advance planning and agreement with the various line managers, but it's a great way to get to know a team. See the section dedicated to this, called *Clothes and Uniforms*.

103

Talent Management

The UK professional body for HR, the Chartered Institute of Personnel and Development (CIPD), states that, 'Talent management seeks to attract, identify, develop, engage, retain and deploy individuals who are considered particularly valuable to an organisation.' (Talent Factsheet published 23.1.20). I disagree with this approach. To single out the elite few and then throw resources at them is not only divisive, but it also ignores the fact that everyone is talented. Many people working in organisations either do not have the opportunity to use their talents, or their talents are suppressed by systems, defined role descriptions and/or culture.

Talent management should be high on every HR professional's agenda. If you can get it right, then you will see a marked increase in productivity, as a direct consequence of giving everyone the chance to play full out. For me, discovering the hidden talents of colleagues has been a real driver for my enjoyment of HR.

How do you find out what talents people have? I argue that it is not about spending money on software that attempts to map everyone's skill set and scores them on their current mastery of the role, and the potential they have, linked to dubious appraisal and marking systems. Instead it is about talking to people, listening to what they say, learning about the things that they do outside work and then giving them regular opportunities to shine.

Opportunities come in many forms just in the HR team: leading or taking part in a project; a short secondment to another area; chairing a meeting; deputising at a meeting; preparing a report; leading a focus group; taking a training programme in a new skill; volunteering as a school governor; illustrating a newsletter; running the pay review; implementing an IT system upgrade; running a training programme; designing a new share scheme, to name but a few.

As an HR leader, a key part of your role is to find a range of ways to encourage people to appreciate and enjoy their talents, and be given the space to flourish. Ignore this at your peril.

For a more comprehensive review of this important subject, I recommend *The Science of Talent*, by Kate O'Loughlin (Panoma Press, 2018). There are several books covering talent management, but this is the first that I've found that is both easy and interesting to read from cover to cover.

104

Team-Building

Often derided by senior managers, who see the words 'team-building' in a diary and instantly associate it with a loss of productivity. When used at appropriate times, however, my belief is that team-building can be one of the best ways to motivate a group and rarely fails to increase productivity as a consequence.

Some people fail at the start by proposing an exotic venue for their meeting. This can embarrass the team and make them feel uncomfortable, trying to explain to their families and work colleagues why they have to travel to a holiday destination for a team meeting. The trick is to think about the venue, which is often way better when off-site, away from the distractions of the normal office or workplace. It can be a treat, just within reason.

Once the location has been chosen, the title for the day then becomes important. Straight team-building evokes visions of colleagues having to walk through pretend minefields or trust each other when falling backwards. Whilst these can have a place in a programme, the headline is better when it reflects the expected output from the day. A strategic planning day, or operational review day can work well, as can a team objective-setting day.

An alternative to a purely work-based approach, is to undertake a charitable activity. Rather than criticism, your team will receive praise, and will feel good about what they have achieved. Local charities often have projects that they want to do, but just don't have the people to make them happen. I've been involved in redecorating a youth space, running a tea party for a care home outing, cleaning out animal pens at a zoo, planting out seedlings in a community allotment after rescuing an overgrown weed patch, producing and distributing a magazine, and partnering with *The Big Issue*.

When I look back at away days which went particularly well, they all had a theme or an output that was later used by the team. They all had involved practical activities, and everyone felt they had contributed. The away days I haven't appreciated, and have often endured, have included large periods of time being talked at, or presented to, with little opportunity for interaction or involvement.

If you do take your team off-site, then don't forget to let other teams know where you're going and what you'll be doing, and have a mechanism in place to handle an urgent incident. This does happen, and I have had to ask a team member to drop out of an away day to resolve a serious problem back at work on more than one occasion.

105

Team Spirit

Maintaining team spirit, a sense of fun and achievement, is part and parcel of running an HR team. Some of the team will want to understand what the strategy going forward is, where the team fits into the larger organisation, what the detailed plans are and how they can manage their time to complete them. Others will just want to turn up, do their job, and go home without taking any responsibilities with them. You need to understand what motivates each member of your team, and then ensure that your communications give them what they need, including recognition for work well done.

The biggest problems I have faced as a line manager of HR teams have nearly always been related to geography, with members split across the country, or even across countries. It's tough to build a team when time zones mean that people are eating breakfast in the States, whilst Team Europe has just had lunch, or Team Asia is about to go home. But it's worth persevering, using video links, running a check-in so that people share their experiences and/or workload, and occasionally do some crazier things, like get one of the team to run a short quiz or similar. I also used to deliberately ask one person from each location to join a small team to work up an idea together and report back to the next meeting, effectively forcing people to work together, often at different levels of experience in the organisation, just to spark a rapport. What that means is that when you do get a chance to meet up in the same location, you're already at a decent stage in forming the team, rather than at start-up.

Another issue to watch out for is where you have some members of the team who regularly travel between sites, whilst other team members are based in the office or their home for five days a week. They see members of the team travelling around, maybe will be a bit jealous about the perceived lifestyle they lead, and wonder what's happening and why things are so rushed when everyone gets back to the office.

Once you are conscious of these issues you can start to tackle them with a series of initiatives. An agreement to not to have external meetings every Monday morning (or other day that works) and for everyone to keep an hour for a catch-up over coffee will at least help with scene-setting and making people feel included. Add to that an occasional full day for a complete team meeting to share and discuss priorities, and you're starting to involve everyone.

A shared electronic diary that the team can see where everyone is each day, preferably at least a week in advance, means that proper messages can be given to others asked their whereabouts. Equally, a WhatsApp group (or similar) where you all just chat briefly about what's happening in the moment can also help with team spirit, although beware that not everyone will want to share their personal phone number with the rest of the group, so an enterprise equivalent running off the work's email may be better.

Regular short emails to the group from the people travelling, such as 'Just met XYZ and it went really well, we need a draft proposal, YES!' can work a treat. Where possible, it is good to encourage the office team to accompany the travellers on their trip on at least one occasion, to get an idea of what happens and the issues faced whilst out and about. In one case I took the person who was responsible for booking travel for me, and after that I was always given more time to transit between planes at terminals.

106

Thank You

It's almost a lost art form, but saying thank you in a genuine way is difficult on email alone. You can make it more impactful by copying in the line manager of the person you're thanking, and making sure that their support for you or your project is properly acknowledged, but I have found that a written card, letter or notelet can be far more powerful. The fact that you have bothered to buy a card, find a pen and write something on it, works well. I think, in part, it also has extra impact because it is no longer the norm, and it will stand out as post from all the marketing brochures, invoices and expense claims. Give it a try. I was pleasantly surprised when I visited accounts payable after about six months, and saw one of my cards still pinned up next to the person who had gone the extra mile to help me that time. I pointed to it, she smiled; nothing more needed to be said.

For a more significant project that has been completed, sending the project team out for a meal or a show can work well, in addition to the more standard bonuses. A lovely touch is to send flowers, or whatever is appropriate (e.g. a nice bottle of something), to the partner of the employee, especially if they have been putting in extra hours to complete a project.

There are some excellent commercial platforms, or portals, which come packaged with benefits programmes, where employees or line managers can nominate special rewards. These can give you a cost-effective way of rewarding team members with a choice that they want (e.g. a parent might prefer the theme park tickets over a night out), but they can be quite 'mechanical', i.e. a nomination is made and then the automated system kicks into action. Hence my comment above about remembering the special touch of a handwritten note, even if it does take a week to get to the project manager working abroad!

107

Trade Unions and Staff Reps

It saddens me to think that so much training for HR people is about how to 'manage' a trade union, how to manage the risks, how to challenge a ballot, understand the law, and to know how many days must elapse before an agreement can be broken, or enforced.

For me the training should be about how to listen to the people who represent your employees, how to respond appropriately, how to encourage them, how to truly engage in meaningful dialogue, how to reach agreement, and how to jointly find ways to improve employee engagement, and hence productivity.

I accept that it is difficult if the elected representatives are either too sycophantic (and essentially just there to apologise on behalf of the employer), or if they are intent on destroying capitalism in any form and/or have an anarchist's agenda. In most cases though, representatives want to see people treated with dignity, earn a fair wage and have reasonable working conditions. Isn't that also the agenda for the HR team, for the management team and for the board?

If you agree that it is a shared agenda, then progress can be made. Instead of seeing everything as points scored, or a win/loss, you instead start sharing ideas, drawing in the representatives under a confidentiality agreement if needed, being daring in how you might progress, whilst being realistic about constraints (money often plays a part).

I view my role in HR as bringing the representatives of the employees closer to the managers of the business and vice versa, not about how to keep them on opposite sides of the ring.

To be successful this involves training the reps in a range of fields: from how to be good representatives; to agree reasonable time off from their normal work with their managers so they can play the role in full; to understanding accounts; to them hearing directly the views of senior leaders and understanding fully the objectives of the organisation.

Something I have said at every rep training and at the start of most meetings that I have run is, 'Remember that you represent the people who elected you. When you speak we will always assume that you are speaking on their behalf, and understand that the views you represent are theirs, and not necessarily yours. Therefore, feel free to speak out. There will not be any reprisals or bad feeling towards you as the representative.'

Equally, of course, the managers should be trained in working with the reps, to actively listen, not to automatically raise objections to every suggestion and to see the bigger picture. Getting managers to attend a training session is near impossible in most companies, so I have usually had to brief each attending manager separately, and this works well when you have rotating leadership reps.

Once the training is complete and you start to hold the first meetings, expect things to be relatively straightforward. People are feeling their way, they're maybe a bit sceptical and they will be unlikely to raise agenda items, so make sure you keep a lot of time for AOB (any other business) and allow pregnant pauses to give people a chance to speak, encouraging those that are more timid.

Your job is to listen carefully and take everything seriously. It is to make sure that every rep gets a chance to contribute (especially if there is a dominant rep – don't forget they may not speak for the majority, so actively seek others' views). To be able to listen fully, you will need a colleague to take minutes of the meeting, if appropriate.

In a small biotech I remember buying some picnic benches and changing the quality of the toilet paper in the early days following requests made; but it was the fact that these things were heard and done that led reps to start raising more important issues as time went by, and trust began to build. From everything happening in AOB, we moved to a full set of issues on the agenda, proposed in advance by the reps themselves.

Hopefully, when a major event is being planned within the business, such as a restructuring, your reps will already be trained and sufficient trust will have built up within the group. If so, then this is the moment to take a leap of faith and tell the reps, in confidence, what is being planned.

At Glaxo we increased meetings from bi-monthly to weekly when a major event was occurring and gave the reps as much information as we could, separating out what they could tell their people from what they had to keep confidential, with explanations as to why. Countless times the feedback that we received changed the way that we ran the process. We were lucky to have an excellent leader of the TU side, who subsequently crossed the line and is now a very successful HR Director.

There is nothing like listening to people who are directly impacted by a change, telling you how they feel about it, and how you can make it as dignified as possible. There is also nothing better than eventually going to the wider employees with a message which you have road-tested with the reps first, and ironed out the management speak.

When national trade unions are involved and have an appropriate representation agreement, then there are some added advantages for the organisation. Often, they will provide excellent rep training, and will have extra resources to call on, sometimes full-time paid staff. In these cases, you need to find time, especially when a major event is happening, to talk with these people. You will learn a lot from them. They are experts in change and will often have some good ideas about how to make the very changes that you want to achieve. Far from blocking things, a full and frank conversation with the TU team can open things up.

At the Medical Research Council, for example, we had access to four different trade unions, and each one made significant and fundamental contributions to the big changes that took place, especially some very complicated TUPE moves. Their head office experts helped us find the best solution for our employee's time and time again, whilst the leader of the MRC TU team played a key role in diplomatically balancing the needs of the business with the needs of his members, a rare skill. The team of TU reps also helped us unlock and progress with dignity the difficult process of accepting volunteers for redundancy, something that senior managers will often fight, fearing that the best will leave. But if you impose redundancies, then the best will leave anyway!

In conclusion I would argue that by working with employees, staff reps and unions, rather than assuming you know what is best for them, you will get better results faster and achieve gains in productivity rather than lost time, lost discretionary effort and lost morale.

Training for Researchers

As mentioned in the Introduction, one of the things that I was proud of when working at Wellcome was the establishment of a major collaborative project with The Open University, which led to the launch of an online suite of training programmes, covering all the key areas that academic and research-based line managers needed to learn. Although it was developed for research scientists, it still has value for everyone who has to manage a team, albeit most of the examples are lab-based. Each module has a modest price, and some you can pass just by showing that you already have appropriate prior learning. If you study all of them you will get a certificate of recognition. Search for 'International Funders Award Open University'.

The course was put together after we realised this was a big unmet need in the science research world, especially after visiting researchers in Africa and Asia who were working miles from a university. Wellcome Trust helped fund the development and support came from the Medical Research Council, Institut Pasteur, Bill and Melinda Gates Foundation and the Biotechnology and Biological Scientific Research Council.

Part of the reason for including this section is to remind everyone heading an HR team that they always need to be thinking about the bigger picture, how can the business be made more efficient, how can productivity be increased. By identifying something as simple as a training need, you can make a big difference.

Travel

One of the best opportunities you will get is to travel abroad, either for work, or for a conference. You may also have the opportunity to work abroad for an extended period of time on a placement or secondment.

For one-off or occasional trips, you must remember that customs and practices in the country that you're visiting will be different. Employment laws will also be different, as will cultural norms, so do your research before you travel. The Foreign and Commonwealth Office has up-to-date advice about travelling, the types of visas needed (you are not going on vacation so beware on this point) and any political or civil unrest issues. There might also be diseases that you need to protect against (malaria, for example, or the requirement in some countries to be vaccinated against yellow fever). Get to know your head of travel to help keep the costs and time spent travelling down, and the enjoyment high.

If you are visiting a workplace, try to find out whether the cultural norm is to bring a small gift with you, or whether that would be frowned upon. Research appropriate forms of greeting, and be prepared for a formal handshake in one place, a slight bow in another and a bear hug in the third! Find out whether you will be expected to pay for meals out, or whether it's 50:50. And always beware that asking someone out for a drink (even a coffee) can be taken as a wrong signal in some places, whereas in others it's an essential part of the business process. Take some business cards with you: there's nothing worse than having to go through a ritual that you can't reciprocate.

Once you've planned for the meetings, and remembered simple things like taking a paper copy of a presentation in case your tech turns out to be incompatible (or there is no signal to download from), then think about adding a day or two to your trip before the meetings start. Unless your travel company can demonstrate that by travelling on a Saturday you have brought the flight costs down, you may have to pay for a couple of extra nights' accommodation, but you will benefit richly from the experience. This way you can explore the city, its culture, its museums, galleries, and eateries at the same time as adjusting to the time zone, so that you are fresh for the meeting.

If you have the opportunity to stay in a country for an extended period of time, try to avoid the temptation of staying exclusively with the expat community (i.e. other people from your home country also living in the host country). Whilst interactions with them will initially help you find your way around, the real value of your stay only begins when you integrate with the local people, go to the places they shop and go for their entertainment, and start living, and understanding, their lives. Get professional help with your tax issues from your company's advisors and ensure that you are not too out of pocket when it comes to your full range of expenses (such as running your base home at a distance if it is not being rented in your absence).

110

Trial Periods

One of the most effective tools I have used throughout my working life is the Trial Period. Why? Because it is the single most effective way of dealing with the conservative forces that exist in most human beings: the desire to maintain the status quo and a quiet life.

The problem is that businesses have to evolve to survive, and sometimes that evolution requires a step change. The art of the Human Resources and Organisational Development person is to find a way for that change to land well with those who work at the organisation.

And that's where several factors come into play. The first is always communication. If you are open and honest and describe the logic behind what you are trying to do, you will start to get the help and support, as opposed to resistance, of your team. Listen to what they say and act by making changes and you will start to engage, and maybe even get a better result than the one originally envisaged by your senior team. Alternatively, steamroller away and then rehire, the choice is yours, but the latter path will be remembered by many for years to come, and some of those will be your customers!

When you need to make changes, you will know there is never one simple answer. So, think about introducing change in chunks and sometimes as a trial. Here's an example: the senior leadership team wants to introduce a greater degree of flexible working. It seems the way to go, everyone else is ahead of the game and your leaders believe that change is needed to remain competitive when hiring. But some are concerned about people abusing the new system and a drop in productivity, others about their fears they will be asked to work longer hours under the guise of flexible working.

Rather than issuing a diktat and a set of new rules, and investing in considerable effort to 'sell' the new package to your employees, why not introduce a trial in an area that is run by a leader who really 'gets it' and another trial in an area managed by someone who doesn't and will resist?

You take the trial teams into a meeting, explain what you're trying to do, how you hope it will work, what you think are the pros and cons (yes, be open), and you ask them to give it a go for, say, three months. After this time you will review the situation, with the option of reverting to the old methods. The conservatives will be thinking, 'This will never work, but we can go back to our old ways in three months', some won't care either way and the rest will want to see how to make it work, because they can now see the benefits.

Two months in, start asking around, and make some tweaks to soften the rough edges. Maybe extend the trial to six months, get other teams involved in their trials of the tweaked version (some will be clamouring for it by now) and before you know it, everyone will be on a trial. You probably won't even need to review it, because the trial will just become the new norm by default, as we have seen with changes made to working life as a consequence of COVID-19.

The above is about teams and even company change, but trial periods are also useful for individuals who are struggling with their role. A trial in a new job, or a new area, or with some coaching, always feels less threatening than a binary decision. For example, in redundancy situations, a particular role will no longer exist when the change is made but there is a vacancy elsewhere. The trial gives the employee and the new line manager the right to give it a go and then say yes or no. It really works well, as long as both sides are supported by the HR team in the early days.

111

Tribunals

Every so often a disgruntled ex-employee or an aggrieved job applicant will refuse to accept an apology, or will fail to negotiate a settlement agreement, insisting on their day in court. Just when you think you have everything under control, an unwelcome letter arrives, explaining that you have a set number of days to respond to the claim being made.

The first check is to see if the claim has been made within the approved time frame from the date of dismissal or the selection decision. If it fails this test, you may well be able to refute it and move on, but the likelihood is that you do have to respond and you need to present your case. When doing so you become what is known as the 'respondent'. Your role is to lay out the facts as you see them, which are likely to be at odds with the version presented by the applicant. You will need to collate all the relevant documents and create a bundle to be presented in advance to the tribunal, and copied to the applicant.

You also need to prepare your witnesses, and that might include yourself. It's key to have an agreed timeline when events occurred, and contemporary notes about the actions taken to refer to. If you are called, then keep your answers short, and always be honest, or at worst, economical with the truth. Your reputation is on the line. There is always a chance that a settlement can be agreed, either through the intervention of ACAS, or even up to the final minutes before the case is about to be heard, between representatives of both sides. It is possible to represent yourself at a tribunal, but companies regularly employ solicitors to do this for them, and even barristers or Queen's Counsel when the stakes are high (such as in discrimination cases, where the awards are unlimited).

If that letter does arrive, and you have not witnessed a tribunal before, look up where the nearest venue is and go along for the day with a packed lunch and something to read (there are always delays and hold-ups; it is not an efficient system). This is an eye-opening experience and invaluable to prepare yourself for what is to come. Tribunals are unlike the court rooms that appear in TV programmes. There is normally a legally qualified chair, an employer and a union representative, dressed smartly, who will hear the case, and have the right to ask questions as the case unfolds. They want to get to a fair result, and put considerable effort into achieving that. You will witness hardened company representatives struggling to justify an event, applicants forgetting what their main reason for attendance is, and any number of lost minutes as people try to find the right document to prove their tenuous point. Appeal hearings are much slicker, and lawyers play a bigger part, but let's hope you never have to go that far into the system.

112

TUPE

In the UK employment market TUPE relates to the transfer (or control) of business, usually services, from one company to another, and what happens to the employees working there. Officially, the acronym stands for Transfer of Undertakings (Protection of Employment) Regulations 2006.

For example, it might be that a contract for the lab services that are provided to a hospital moves from one outsource provider to another, or that a company decides to outsource a service, like IT, currently provided by employees.

Under the TUPE regulations, the main terms and conditions of the people who hold the jobs in the group which is being moved are protected (e.g. pay and holidays won't be any worse, and sometimes improve). The exception is pension plans, which are held outside of TUPE.

When the transfer occurs, employment moves from one organisation to the other, and this includes the provision of a P45, which can be quite scary unless it is explained in advance to the staff concerned.

Once the business has made a decision to undertake a transfer, it is key that the HR teams from both parties get together as soon as possible. Communications and consultation should be top of the list, alongside the mechanics of the transfer. These days it is likely that one party will have experience, and often it is the acquiring organisation. Either they will provide an experienced TUPE project manager or you will agree that an experienced interim is required. Never underestimate the amount of additional work that a TUPE entails. Where the employment terms are markedly different or the numbers are large, you might also need the support of an employment lawyer. Make sure there is a budget that covers all these items (indeed one TUPE I was involved in never happened after the director discovered the full costs and implications, and a small restructuring occurred instead).

Initially the project manager will need support preparing the plan, understanding the issues, meeting key stakeholders, getting set up on both IT systems, drafting initial communications and briefing the line managers alongside the directors and HR team members. If you have a staff consultative group, or trade unions, involve them (in confidence) as soon as you can. If trade unions are involved, then their regional or head office teams might well be able to help with getting the process right. Once ready an all-hands communication, preferably face to face, is needed to formally start the consultation process.

When first alerted to the possibility (or probability) of a TUPE transfer, all but the most robust team members will need reassurance. They will have lots of questions and they will want to meet their new employers early on, to hear from them and start to understand what it will be like working for them. If you can get this right, then chances are only a few people will start seeking alternative employment with other companies. A small in-house team might even be attracted by the prospect of working for a larger specialist company, and therefore being able to access new opportunities for training and development, as well as promotion and working on other sites. In other words, it can be a relatively easy sell, provided you are open and honest from the start.

Throughout the process, consultation on the back of good communications will continue to dominate your agenda. People don't like surprises, so don't hold back, especially if there is some bad news about terms and conditions changing. Instead front up and explain what the alternative is, or why in the round this is still a better deal (unless it isn't, in which case major on-job retention is the main outcome). Make sure that all the correct formal letters are sent at the right stages, and be ready for some appeals or grievances, and listen carefully to them. Occasionally, you will have made a mistake and can use this as a reason to make changes; pride should play no part in your decision-making.

On the day of the transfer, encourage the receiving company to lay out the welcome mat and make their new employees feel warmly welcomed. Agree to review the process once completed and learn from it for any future changes. Thank, and where appropriate, bonus those people who have put in an extra shift to make the transfer successful. Once the transfer is complete the new company may want to make changes to the structure of the team. From now on your role is to support and re-enforce the changes; resisting them will cause unnecessary angst, unless what is happening goes against prior agreements made.

Turnover

I always remember some of my early college lecturers becoming animated about the means you should employ to reduce turnover (debating at length the pros and cons of pay rises and counter-offers to those resigning). They seemed to be working on the basis that very low, or no, turnover was the ultimate goal of any people strategy that an HR team would put in place, namely the old Japanese model, where you start at a company when you leave school and retire from the same company. And yet, I would argue that a reasonable level of turnover (between 5 and 10%) can actually be quite healthy. It allows people in the organisation to grow and develop, hopefully with some being promoted and therefore being retained, that might otherwise have left. It also allows new talent, new ideas, new ways of doing things, to be brought into the organisation.

Turnover data should be looked at with the eye of a sceptic. Don't spend loads of money on software or loads of time trying to calculate it. It's a crude measure and needs to be used as a talking point, not as a tool to hit people with (e.g. reduce turnover from 30 to 20% to get a bonus this year). If you only look at turnover on a whole organisation basis, you will not get a true picture. Five per cent for a company of 1,000 people could actually be hiding 20% turnover in one department. So, take a deep dive every so often.

If you're going to use the data to make a point, or write a report, then the first thing to check is how it is being calculated. You don't want an exec or board member pointing out an error on slide two, thus throwing your whole report into disrepute. The simplest measure is to count the number of people who have left over a year and then divide by the average number of people employed in the group you are reviewing (either add together the number on payroll each month and then divide by twelve, or add the number employed at the start and end of the period and divide by two).

Once you have spotted the areas of concern, review the exit interview notes, or if they don't exist, then the letters of resignation. No luck? Then you might need to make some calls to leavers and see if they will give you some data. Glassdoor might also help here, both gruntled and disgruntled employees use it to write TripAdvisor-style comments about your company. You will need to understand a bit about why people are leaving. There is a huge difference between people leaving because a competitor is paying 20% higher wages across the road, rather than everyone is trying to get away from a particular line manager, or type of work that is being undertaken.

In my experience turnover comes in waves, and is often triggered when a popular member of a team leaves. Not necessarily a good manager; sometimes it can be a smart team member who goes elsewhere. It unsettles people, it makes them wonder if they too should be moving on to better their career, or if they could be earning more money. It's a natural thing and something we need to accept, then move on. The grass isn't always greener on the other side, and I've seen a powerful retention impact occur when a good leaver has returned, and spread the word that actually, this place isn't so bad after all.

If you do identify what you think is an issue that needs to be tackled, don't resolve it as if it is a precise science. We are talking about human behaviour. A great phrase to use is 'I've been taking a look at the turnover levels in this department and when compared to the others, they seem quite high. From a first look at the data that's available, it's my perception that...' By not stating you know what the exact issue is, that it is only your perception (which can be changed), you are keeping the dialogue open and inviting the senior leader to become engaged in the conversation, and probably take ownership of it.

Where you have higher levels of turnover or discontent of any kind, remember the Hawthorne experiments, in which individuals modify aspects of their behaviour when they become aware they are being watched. By simply paying some interest to a department or division you can improve morale (as the researchers did by playing with the lighting levels). The best way to do this is to be open and honest. Pull a group together, maybe bribe them with coffee and cakes, or the promise that it is instead of their weekly Zoom team update, and say that you've noticed quite a few people have left in the past year and you want to understand a bit more what it's like working in the department, and you'd like to listen to ideas to make the work more interesting (or whatever is the initial presenting issue). Ask them to describe what 'great' would look like. Then to describe what it's like now. Instantly, you have a gap, and you can debate with them how to close the gap. Simples! After this meeting, make sure to follow through so people can see something happen, otherwise your bolt is shot.

114

Volunteering

If you are keen to progress either in your current organisation through promotion, or via some strategic sideways moves, or you want to leave for a bigger job elsewhere, then the faster you can build your armoury of skills and experiences the better. And often the easiest way to do that is to volunteer.

Whenever new projects come up in the organisation, think about offering yourself up to take on some additional work. Whether it is to arrange a social event, get involved in a cross-department project, or implement a new software suite, it matters not. Others will see that you are engaging in the lifeblood of the organisation and they will notice.

Don't limit yourself to internal opportunities; keep an eye open in your local community. You can learn a lot by being the governor of a local school, by being trained as a Samaritan, by running a youth sports team or by cooking for the homeless. Your local library will sometimes have opportunities that don't make it onto the internet, so ask around. They may also be able to link you with local charities that need non-exec board members, the experience of which will help in the future when you want to take up a paid role as a non-executive director.

In the wider context, volunteering can be used to develop teams in the workplace. Some community-based projects need help on an occasional basis to do things like redecorate a community centre, make tea and scones for the elderly, escort a group with disabilities to the park or museum, work on a community vegetable plot – the list is endless.

At Wellcome Trust we had the benefit of working with an excellent facilitator, who had a gift for matching volunteers with projects needing support. She made a huge difference. Make the arrangements with the community project organisers, run a risk analysis with your health and safety team, then get volunteering! Even in the pouring rain, every team that I have ever had a volunteering day with has thoroughly enjoyed themselves, they have bonded, they have done something useful, and they have been thanked by their bosses for bringing some good publicity to the organisation (remember to take photos to send to the local press as well as using social media).

Wellbeing

If you have an employee committee, then wellbeing is a wonderful project for them to get involved in. And I say that because wellbeing isn't something that you can impose on a work environment: you need active involvement from many different people for it to be a success.

If you don't have an employee council or similar, then send round a communication to everyone, inviting those with an interest in wellbeing to attend an initial meeting where you can explain what you want to achieve, and then ask for people to volunteer, possibly as Wellbeing Champions. This is a non-onerous task, which involves only occasional meetings, maybe over sandwiches, in which they canvass ideas from their teams and share them in the forum. It's also something they can add to their CVs.

At the first meetings run some sessions to generate ideas, get people to talk to their friends and find out what is happening elsewhere. If you get lots of offers of help, split them up into groups to cover different aspects, such as mental health, physical wellbeing, dietary health and financial health. And who knows: maybe the wellbeing team will morph into a staff committee over time as they discuss issues that need to be resolved in the organisation.

Don't worry about a wellbeing policy, just start doing stuff. And the great thing is that you won't need a big budget, nor extended time off, as most people will happily take part in activities during their own time.

Working in Africa

It isn't possible to write this chapter without stating upfront that Africa is a collection of many different countries, often created in a way that had no respect for tribal boundaries, by Europeans withdrawing from occupation in the twentieth century. What this means is that some countries will forever be troubled by containing different ethnic groups, with proud histories, that can't comfortably sit around a table with each other. Uganda is one such place, and the need to be respectful of culture as a visitor (especially when working there), is crucial.

Poverty, often caused by the catastrophic impact of climate on crops, goes hand in hand with excessive wealth, and can be witnessed in most countries in Africa. Expats often live in secure compounds protected by high fences and security, showering in hot water whilst maids cook their food, just a few hundred metres from shanty towns of shacks with corrugated iron roofs, where people have to walk half a mile for 'fresh' water pumped from a well. These things need to be said, because if you work in Africa you cannot ignore them. You need to understand them. For example, a signal from head office to restructure and reduce the wage bill by 10% in Europe, might mean a few people receiving redundancy pay and having to move jobs, whilst in Africa it can mean whole families going without food and medical provisions.

Each country has its own interesting features and working style. In the Gambia, for example, I learned the hard way that when a driver said he would pick me up at one, it meant one hour after sunrise, not 1 pm. Being close to the equator, that was around 8 am, but because of the state of the roads and never being sure exactly what was happening, 8 am was always give or take thirty minutes. The polar opposite of Switzerland, where I once booked a taxi for 8 am. It arrived at 07:59:55 and left at 08:00:55. I wasn't in it, because I hadn't allowed for the ninety seconds' walk from reception to the taxi rank!

The other surprise for me, working in Africa, was the fact that I looked like a right idiot dressed in my easy wicking shirts and khaki trousers. I struggled with the heat and humidity, but, of course, everyone I met was fully adjusted to the climate and wore standard business attire, dark trousers, shirts, often jackets. Gifts were never a big feature, but the chance to chat and have a sugary coffee or tea were highly prized, and I learned a lot by just listening and trying to understand the world from their perspective. It rarely aligned with what was being proposed in London. A desire to send out more -80C freezers from head office was challenged by the guys on the ground saying that their generators wouldn't be able to cope with the extra load (there being no continuous reliable mains electricity available), and that what was really needed was an upgrade to the internet (a few hours a day was all that was possible, with very slow upload speeds for reports, etc).

On the map, Malawi is relatively close to South Africa, but you can only guess at the differences that you experience when travelling between one and the other. The people I met and worked with in Malawi were, without question, the most humble and wonderfully generous people, and yet they lived in one of the poorest countries in the world. Nothing was too much trouble and they were proud and lovely. Quite a contrast to the big cities in South Africa, where large investments have been made and the country is still coming to terms with tremendous political and social change. I don't think it is easy to prepare yourself for trips to places like this; no amount of reading tourist guide books helps. If the chance comes, grab it, and be prepared to learn a lot in a short period of time. Make sure that you add time at the front and back of the trip to explore and spend money in the local markets, rather than at the airport on the way home.

117

Working in India

I was lucky to share some exceptional trips to India with work colleagues, as we selected companies to partner with, checking the ethical standards and conditions in their laboratories and factories were appropriate, before deals were signed for the supply of reagents and potential drug candidates.

India is a huge country, and each state has its individual people, customs, laws and ways of operating. It also has endless levels of bureaucracy, which we can blame on the occupying forces from the UK. Once I spilled some food on a shirt that I needed to wear for a dinner. The hotel receptionist refused to take it from me and said that a porter would fetch it from my room. The porter arrived, pulled out a pad, and proceeded to press down very hard with a biro through fifteen layers, which included the tatty blue carbon paper, to produce eight copies. I was given the bottom copy, which had a very faint outline of what had been ordered. I have no idea where all the other copies were sent to. But I do know that the super express two-hour service took forty-eight hours. And thankfully I could buy a better shirt at a decent price in the shop next door. Indeed, porters were quite a feature of our trip, always springing up whenever we moved, offering to carry a bag or a case, or even an envelope, for a small tip in return. Remember to carry plenty of small change with you when you go (US currency is best).

And so to business. Or, as the trip unfolded, how many drinks could you refuse before relenting and either having a local beer or a Johnnie Walker whisky? This was especially the case in the 'dry' states, where a visiting delegation from Britain was a special excuse to open the bar and offer drinks to every director and manager in the building, or so it seemed!

Exchanging small gifts was hit and miss. We took them in bags just in case, and only presented them when we needed to. Handshakes and pleasantries over, we were always surprised by how much they already knew about us. Indeed, some of the things they knew felt like they could only have come from colleagues in companies we had visited in another state the day or week before. Maybe there was an intricate web of data flowing, or each company employed excellent spies, we were never sure, but we were careful not to discuss business in the cars they provided to move us between meetings. And a tip about cars: it's best to ask for a driver who is not a fatalist.

Deals were tough to negotiate, but business moved fast, and in one case, they had set up videoconferences for the day we returned to the UK to begin the scientific discussions. Over the next few months, time zones worked in our favour. We could ask for a test to be run at the close of business in the UK evening, knowing that they would be five and a half hours ahead and have the result when we logged into the system in the UK morning.

118

Working in Japan

My experience of working with colleagues in Japan was far less than that working with colleagues in the USA, Africa or Europe, but it did make a profound impression on me. Whilst unique is an overused word that I should avoid, my first visit to Japan was certainly exactly that: it wasn't the incomprehensible instructions on the toilets, which meant that instead of flushing them, I ended up spraying myself, turning up the heat or even making weird musical noises; nor was it the incredibly beautiful and delicate foods, which I had already had some exposure to (albeit there is a world of difference between freshly prepared sushi and the stuff you get in lunch boxes in London cafés); instead it was the people. Unbelievably friendly, way too helpful and overly respectful. Bowing, apologising, trying to make everything perfect all the time, giving presents at every opportunity and ensuring that no minute of my time in the country was underused.

After a few hours I was beginning to want someone to answer back, or question my motives. It felt like I was taking advantage of people. I wanted to open a door, or pay for something myself; it almost felt suffocating. But the biggest shock was yet to come. Workwise, I really thought we were getting some traction and reaching an agreement, but it was simply my counterparts trying to be polite and not offend me. There was no expectation of actually doing any business on day one. Or day two. Or even week two. These lovely people wanted to study us and see whether we were fly-by-night, or there to stay. Making things happen was a new glacial level of slow, quite the opposite from my US trips.

I also learned early on that, in general, the Japanese don't ever want to be seen to lose face. When I was asked for my opinion on something, I learned not to give my opinion, in case it caused offence, but instead to give something I disliked faint praise. This had already been applied to performance measures in the labs. The equivalent of a UK 'underperforming, needs improvement', in Japan would be 'performing', which would translate to the same 0% pay increase in the UK. In other words, everything was ratcheted up a notch. It was also clear that everyone I was speaking to had been in their company since college, and felt a strong loyalty to their leader. So different to the US and Europe, where people tend to move between organisations to achieve personal development and growth.

My experiences above were as the employee of a company that had developed interests in Japan. It was, therefore, different to the experiences of both my family and friends who have worked for Japanese companies in Japan or Europe. Hierarchy is the word that I hear them use again and again. Suggestions for improvements in productivity which come from the shop floor rarely get high enough up the chain of command to be implemented, and often results are presented in such a good light that unprofitable goods or practices keep running way beyond their expected lifespan. All of this is completely at odds with the stereotype of kaizen, the concept of constantly improving things at a small scale.

If you are about to do business in Japan, or with Japanese companies, my advice is that you seek out professional advice early on. Don't think you can wing it.

119

Working for a Japanese Company

This Chapter is written by Sarah Collins, as I have no expertise in this field, and yet it needs to be understood.

When I started working in the European office of a Japanese company, I was told it would be different to working for other companies, but it took me a while to understand why. Initially I saw that 95% of the staff were European, and only a handful were Japanese. The CEO of Europe was European. Other than addressing people with '-san' after their name, not much looked different.

Interestingly, the Japanese team members sat in on many of the meetings, said little in most cases, but wrote a lot. I learned that this information was being relayed to the headquarters in Japan. After a while I got used to this and carried on as normal. I discovered that the longstanding traditions and cultures of Japan influence how business is done. The ways of doing business, decision-making through committee, with everything done slowly to ensure that that the long-term impact was fully assessed, was commonplace.

I learned to play the long game and start projects that needed buy-in well ahead of time. I learned that listening, contemplating and then responding was the wisest way of operating. For someone who in Myers-Briggs terms is an E (Extrovert) and N (Intuitive), this was a personal challenge. I also learned to always have business cards with me wherever I went, and to pass these with two hands; not to put cards I had received away, but to display these on the table in front of me; to bow; to wait to be seated at meetings, so the most senior could sit first, and in the seats furthest from the door.

My first meetings with my Japanese colleagues taught me that for them I was the odd one out. I had specialised in HR all of my career. Specialisation doesn't typically happen in Japanese companies. Most are hired as graduates, usually into a sales role, and then they progress through all areas of the business, learning all the different disciplines. This gives them great breadth and understanding of the whole organisation, and plays a key role in forming part of the learning culture that exists in life-long-term employment for the Japanese.

This provides a great opportunity for Europeans and Americans, if we wish to take it, to get involved in global projects, because the depth of knowledge we have – whether that is about global performance management, or system selection and implementation, and everything in-between – they do not have in depth, and so are interested to learn from. Life-long learning is a key theme and can work in both directions if you are willing to be patient, and accept the relatively slow pace these projects move at.

A major set of learnings for me came alongside the annual assessment of business performance, and the performance of the senior team, in the year that the European business was without a CEO. HR is seen as an important partner behind the CEO, so much of this fell to me. In this process I learned:

- The value of a detailed briefing pack of all possible data that might be needed by the visiting Japanese team, needed to be sent well in advance. This enabled preparatory meetings in Japan to take place and for much of the decision-making to be done before they travelled.
- Merit and achievement as drivers for pay, performance, promotion and praise are not the only drivers in Japan. Values, be-

haviours, age and gender all play a part. Little praise is given; instead the focus is on where to improve.

- When some of the European country MDs presentations failed to meet the expectations of the Japanese team, they were not given clear communication as to why. Minimal feedback was provided, but it was subtle and often led to misunderstandings as people did not read between the lines correctly.

- I was often joined by a mid-ranking Japanese team member who was on international assignment. He became 'my shadow'. We talked often, analysed much and of course the information was shared with head office, but I actually found this relationship invaluable and I learned a lot. I would say if this scenario happens to you, see it as a positive and embrace it; it has the potential to work, but always be aware of those subtleties in the feedback, and make sure you don't miss any of the cues given.

Working in the USA

'We have really everything in common with America nowadays, except, of course, language.'

The Canterville Ghost by Oscar Wilde, 1887

When I was working at Glaxo I was given the chance to run a project with the US team in North Carolina, and I discovered the truth of both Oscar Wilde's statement above, and the better-known quote attributed to George Bernard Shaw in the 1940s that 'The United States and Great Britain are two countries separated by a common language.'

My first taste was in Greenford, West London. I went down to reception to meet a couple of American colleagues who had just flown into Gatwick and been driven straight into work. When I arrived, the receptionist explained that they had to go to their hotel for a bath. I was confused, not least because the hotel booking was for that evening. Would they even get a room in this busy season?

Half an hour later I found out. They were confused! All they had asked was if they could use the bathroom. The receptionist didn't understand American English. If only they had asked for the toilet, the loo or the WC, they would have been fine. But this story doesn't end there. About a year later a similar incident was saved by the taxi driver, who explained to the receptionist that a rest room was not a bedroom in a hotel, but was also another name for a toilet. Clearly people need to watch more American films and sitcoms.

On my first trip to Research Triangle Park in North Carolina, I started noticing signs on doors. At the main entrance to the research labs there was a sign asking that all guns be handed in at reception. And then as we walked through to HR, I was dumbfounded by a notice on the door of the occupational health suite. It read: *Free shagging lessons: book inside*. This was before Austin Powers had helped educate everyone, and I was immediately thinking that the occupational health team wanted to encourage safe sex amongst the researchers. If you're not aware, in American English, shagging is a form of swing dancing or jitterbug in the Carolinas, not the other version of catching a fly ball in a baseball game, or the UK version which involves two people becoming very close indeed.

But my biggest problem was yet to come. On this trip my first task was to give a series of presentations. To get things right I decided to rehearse with a critical audience and invited some of the US HR team to come and listen and ask questions, as I tried out my presentation. The EA had booked a great room; it was serviced with a large bowl of popcorn and a hundred different cans of fizzy drinks, all in ice (just what do the Americans think when they turn up in the UK and have to remember to bring their own water?).

I set myself up. Nerves kicked in and the burst of adrenaline overpowered my jet lag. I gave what I thought was an excellent talk. There were a few questions. I then reminded them that I had to repeat this talk four times the next day to the scientists and asked for feedback. The first three all told me it was 'quite good', and then added a few small things to change, e.g. the spelling of 'colour' to 'color'.

I was devastated. That night I spent several hours when I should have been sleeping, rewriting the presentation. And the next day one of the HR volunteers sat in on my first presentation, which I thought went okay, but wasn't as good as the old one. At the end I asked her 'Was that any better?' And she said, 'I don't know why you changed it; it was great before.'

I was still jet lagged. It took me a few minutes to realise that 'quite good' in North Carolina English meant 'very good' when translated to UK English. Jeez! That was a hard way to learn.

Looking back, it's interesting to think that cultural awareness courses were run for people travelling to Africa and Asia, but not for a business trip to the States. To be fair, I remember being warned not to make any form of physical contact with anyone in the States, unless it was a handshake, for fear of being charged with assault. This turned out to be poor advice as some of my hosts later explained that they had been trained to expect full hugs and continental kisses, and so thought that we were formal and stuffy when we first arrived.

My next shock happened that evening. I'd gone back to my hotel to catch up on emails and phone home, and then ventured out at 8 pm for some food, but everywhere was closing. In the US, evening meals peak around 6 pm, which explains why my American colleagues suffer so much when they travel to Spain and Italy and have to wait until 9 pm for the first restaurants to open. I made do with a club sandwich at the hotel (another disappointment, it said it came with 'chips' but in American English that turned out to be 'crisps').

One big danger for Brits travelling to the US on business, is to think that the USA is one country. My experience is that it isn't. Each State has its own character, its own culture and its own ways of doing business. Indeed, most States are so large that they each have many subsets of culture and norms. Whilst I found the North Carolinians genuinely friendly (relaxed, happy to small talk and even invite you to their home for supper), I later found the Philadelphians brusque, sometimes arrogant, wanting to get straight to business, agree the deal and move on (imagine them in Japan trying to do a deal at speed) and the New Yorkers and Californians a mix of everything. In the States, you have to adapt to the person in front of you, and not make any assumptions at all.

When I was working two weeks at a time, or more, I would explore the country at the weekends. I learned not to stop at highway bars where the car park ('parking lot') was filled exclusively with pick-up trucks. I learned that it was best to leave just before the end of an ice hockey game and to buy drinks for veterans attending Army vs Duke football games. I learned that college sports were of a higher standard than professional games in Europe. I learned that when ice rain came, you stopped driving immediately, and when a tornado warning came on the radio, you drove as fast as you could to the next bridge and hid under it.

I also learned that each State has its own employment practices and laws and requirements. If you are hiring, as we did, sales reps in different States, then each needs their own payroll and their own registration process, and often separate benefits packages. It's why it is simpler, when starting out, to use a company that specialises in payroll and benefits programmes across all the States to set you up and get you going. You will save hours of time and trouble, and avoid the potential for fines. Believe me on this one! The cost of working with a payroll partner is tiny compared to going it alone.

Back to the working environment. In more recent times I have seen the devastation that can be caused by a pushy, hardcore, profit-orientated American arriving in Britain and wanting to change everything to their own style overnight. It's just not possible to carry the people with you if you don't build their trust first. They have feet and will walk if they feel they are not being listened to. Doing what is best for the 'stockholders' (translation: 'shareholders'), like 'laying off' people at will, forgets that the experience and knowledge of the organisation lies inside the minds of those very people. Fire one and another will walk before they are pushed, and they are always the best ones. Equally, people give their best when they feel valued above the KPI.

What have been my learnings? To love the diversity of life and people and not make assumptions, and to always summarise a business meeting at the end to ensure we have agreement on what we decided, so that I don't end up reworking everything at a later date.

Theories X, Y and Z

Even if, like me, you didn't enjoy learning the theory of human resources at college, and prefer the practical side of solving problems, making interventions and facilitating change, it is important to keep a few theories in mind, especially since some of the line managers you work with will have either read all the theories, or will have attended a management development programme that covered them. Knowing the basics is all you need, and Wikipedia is useful for providing an answer to each theory that you have to check upon when asked by a leader. If Wiki whets your appetite, then find the original text and read that. Every so often you will be able to add to your knowledge and become a better advisor in so doing.

Aside from Runciman's Theory of Relative Deprivation, I have probably quoted and used Maslow's Hierarchy of Needs more than any other piece of work. It's simple, and you see it in action every day of your working life. Just when you think it has no place, along comes a virus like COVID-19 and it reminds you just how important Maslow's reflections were.

Zombies

You might think, somewhat uncharitably, that I have added this section to ensure that the book runs from A to Z, but the truth is that zombies exist in many larger organisations, and they cause a significant amount of lost productivity. Zombies are those people that have plateaued in the organisation. They turn up every day, often with a substantial sickness absence record, do the minimum that is required to retain their job, add little or no life to the organisation, and never complain when they get an average performance rating or award. Typically they eat at their desks and always have an excuse to avoid any kind of social event. They work on the basis that if they keep their heads down and keep out of the limelight, never volunteering for anything, that they will survive any structural changes and keep earning their wage until they retire.

If zombies can manage to stay hidden in a big organisation, then fair play to them, but that is rarely the case, and they are often spotted by their colleagues: people who are working hard, putting in the discretionary effort, and who are genuinely annoyed that the zombies keep their jobs and pay when doing so little. If you allow the zombies to remain in place then you are complicit in the lost productivity that they cost you, both directly and indirectly.

In the past, leaders of large organisations have taken different types of action to remove the zombies. Most famously, Jack Walsh, CEO at General Electric, advocated the bottom performing 10% of staff should be dismissed each year. That is certainly one way to tackle the issue, but it does mean you have to have robust measurement systems in place, or a healthy budget to cover your legal costs and/or settlement agreements if you are operating in Europe rather than the United States. Alternatives are many and include: rotation of jobs; people working in different areas of the business; secondments both inside and outside the organisation; active involvement of all staff in projects that run in addition to their normal day job; sabbatical leave to refresh; organisation-led volunteering initiatives (e.g. team building on projects in the community); training and development opportunities to suit all (not just the traditional programmes, but also bite-size and online, costs and time off covered); and training for your line managers in how to spot a zombie, and how to re-invigorate them!

ACKNOWLEDGEMENTS

If you want a job done well, hire an experienced professional. They might charge more per hour, but they are likely to get through the process much faster, and by using their many years of experience they can help you convert a decent effort into a proper finished project. I'm not talking about HR and OD this time, but about the dark art of editing, as a prelude to my huge vote of thanks to Bryony Sutherland, editor extraordinaire. In her summary Bryony notes that I have 'an unhealthy addiction to hyphens and a predilection towards excitable punctuation in general'. My friends who suffer my messages and emails will recognise this, I'm sure. Thankfully, Bryony battled through it and helped present this published version, which is much more readable than when it started out.

A special thanks to guest authors of sections in this book, once long-suffering colleagues, and now special friends, Natasha Gordon and Sarah Collins.

I was helped with my research for the book by Aidan Kiely, Kyra Bransom, Hanah, Sue, Natalie, Mary and Julian. (Full names withheld at their request).

I was encouraged to start writing by Kate O'Loughlin and Andrew Machon, and to keep going when it got tough by Tracy, Tom, James and Liz Smith.

To become the person who could write this book, I have an important group of people to acknowledge, as they helped me become the person that I am.

Sir Richard Sykes, Simon Sturge and Sir John Savill were exceptional CEOs at Glaxo, RiboTargets and the MRC. They gave me the wings to experiment and succeed.

Sally-Louise Smith, Rebecca Leigh and Terry McDonald became one of the highest performing teams I have ever been part of at the MRC as we fought the machine, and won.

Zoe Roberts, Kate Arkless Gray, Emily Bakosi, Mary Bennett and Chris Newstead shone in the field of communications, helping reach parts that other communicators couldn't touch, and being the ones to tell me when I was metaphorically wearing no clothes.

Putting on uniforms and getting to meet people in the wider workforce requires support from amazing people like Claire Adams, Simona Howard Willis, Alan Aldridge, Steve Mason, Rod Richardson and Femke Waltman.

Hiring great people is never easy, but four headhunters stand above the crowd: Ann Gales, Natalie Allen, Caroline Clarke and Tarquin Bennet Coles.

As I learned all about HR in my early years, I shared great experiences with some excellent people and learned lots from them, not least Joanne Beaton, Mike Linnane, Gordon Dawes, Kath Durrant, Charleen Darlington, Carroll Whitney, Mark Taylor, Sarah Rowley, Steve Graham, Tina Miller and Rollin Burhans.

In my last few years in a corporate HR environment, standout team members who suffered cake and coffee once too often include Sam Carford, Kerry Jaycock, JC Fonfreyde, Sherry Charlton, Anusha Everson, Sarah Casemore, Glenn Foster, Lauren Couch and Niki Taigel.

And finally, I met Valentina Rinaldi when she was hired to work as a barista on the fifth floor of the Wellcome Trust building in Euston (see the chapter on coffee). During the COVID-19 lockdown in Italy, she couldn't ply her trade, so she kindly offered to provide an illustration for this book, as well as for *The Train Blog* (published in aid of the NHS Charities and available on Amazon), several children's stories about *Willie the Hippo* for Save the Children, and more. But that's a story for another day. The Snakes and Ladders concept was created with help from a long time friend, the very creative Director of #prcompany, Alyson Essex.

Ted Smith is a senior human resource and organisational development consultant, currently working as MD at UKHR.com Ltd. Ted has a degree in science, a diploma in HRM, and has held positions at Glaxo, Nielsen, Vernalis, the Medical Research Council and Wellcome Trust. He's worked in Europe, USA, Africa and Asia at executive and board level, and is currently chair of the Ideas Foundation (a charity). Ted is the author of The Train Blog: Odd and Weird People-Watching (2020), and has published several children's stories, including The Exploding Turnips, Arthur Ramsbottom and the Dinkle Donkle, and the Willie the Hippo series.

Printed by BoD™in Norderstedt, Germany